NATIONAL GEOGRAPHIC

**OUR WORLD**

STUDENT'S BOOK **6**

### SERIES EDITORS
JoAnn (Jodi) Crandall
Joan Kang Shin

### AUTHOR
Kate Cory-Wright

NATIONAL GEOGRAPHIC
LEARNING

Australia · Brazil · Mexico · Singapore · United Kingdom · United States

**NATIONAL GEOGRAPHIC**

# OUR WORLD

## Let's sing! TR: B44

This is our world.
Everybody's got a song to sing.
Each boy and girl.
This is our world!

I say 'our', you say 'world'.
Our!
World!
Our!
World!

I say 'boy', you say 'girl'.
Boy!
Girl!
Boy!
Girl!

I say everybody move …
I say everybody stop …
Everybody stop!

This is our world.
Everybody's got a song to sing.
Each boy and girl.
This is our world!

# Exciting Sports

**In this unit, I will ...**
- discuss extreme sports.
- discuss safety in sports.
- describe people and actions.
- write a biographical paragraph.

**Look, tick and write.**

1. How do you think these people feel?

   ◯ really happy

   ◯ very worried

   ◯ extremely excited

2. Would you ever do this sport?

3. Write a caption for the photo.

**1** **Listen and read.**

**2** **Listen and repeat.**

These days many young people do dangerous and exciting sports called 'extreme sports'. They can be done in the air, in the water or on land.

Extreme skiers reach speeds of 240 kilometres (150 miles) an hour and fly the **length** of two football fields before they **land**! Another popular land sport is BMX (bicycle **motocross**). In skiing and BMX, people **flip** in the air, like this skier!

**Kitesurfing** is a new kind of surfing. An athlete travels skilfully across the water at speeds of 55 kilometres (35 miles) an hour or more. If he isn't **skilful**, he'll **crash**. Kitesurfers, called 'Charlie Browners', need lots of **strength** in their arms.

**Hang-gliding** is one of the most popular extreme sports, although the **equipment** is expensive. Serious **accidents** are not common, but sometimes people get **injuries** when they land. Imagine flying like a bird at a **height** of 6,000 metres (20,000 feet)!

flip

skiing

kitesurfing

hang-gliding

height

length

land

**3** **Work with a friend.**
What did you learn? Ask and answer.

What are kitesurfers called?

Charlie Browners.

**4** **Listen, read and sing.** TR: A4

# Extreme Sports

*A kitesurfer surfs the waves.*
*A kitesurfer moves with the wind.*
*I've kitesurfed in my dreams*
*ever since I was young!*

**Extreme sports.**
**Flying high in the air!**
**Other sports**
**don't compare!**

**Extreme sports.**
**Look around.**
**They're everywhere!**
**Really exciting sports!**

*Skiers somersault skilfully*
*incredibly high over the snow.*
*I've skied in my dreams*
*ever since I was young!*

**CHORUS**

*Motocross and hang-gliding,*
*are incredibly fun!*
*I've dreamt of doing both*
*ever since I was young!*

**CHORUS**

**5** **Answer the questions.**

1. Circle two types of extreme sports athletes in the song.

2. Underline two extreme sports.

3. Write an extreme sport you would like to try.

St Christoph, Arlberg, Austria

Kitesurfing **has been** popular for about 15 years.
Surfing and skateboarding **have been** popular since the 1970s.
How long **have** you **done** extreme sports?

**for**: for 15 years / for five years / for a month / for an hour
**since**: since the 1970s / since I was born / since June / since last year

**6** **Read.** Write and underline.

| | |
|---|---|
| ~~be~~ | be |
| be | have |
| be | want |

1. Kitesurfing _____has been_____ popular **for** / <u>**since**</u> I was a child.

2. Surfing _____ my favourite sport **for** / **since** many years.

3. Many people _____ accidents **for** / **since**

   kitesurfing began.

4. Skiing _____ my dad's favourite sport **for** / **since** the

   last 20 years.

5. He _____ to become a surfer **for** / **since** he

   was three years old.

6. BMX (motocross) _____ in the Olympics

   **for** / **since** 2008.

**7** **Make sentences.** Use one word in each column.

|  |  |  |
|---|---|---|
| know | in this town | |
| have | a computer | |
| live | the piano | |
| study | skateboarding | for |
| play | English | since |
| | best friend | |
| | a bicycle | |
| | football | |
| | in this street | |

**8** **Work in a group.** Discuss. Compare your sentences from Activity 7. Are they the same or different?

How long have you had a bike?

I've had a bike for five years.

I've had one for three years.

**9** **Listen and repeat.** Then read and write. TR: A6

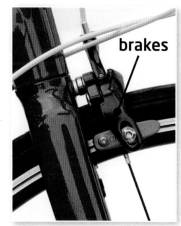

a life jacket

1. Most skateboarding injuries happen when people do tricks and fall on the hard ground. Protect your elbows by wearing _____.

2. If you practise water sports, you might fall in the water. Wear a bright _____ on your body, even if you can swim.

3. When you go cycling or skateboarding, always protect your knees by wearing _____.

4. Check your bicycle _____ often! If they work well, you can stop your bicycle quickly.

5. BMX riders often have accidents. They should wear a _____ so that if they fall, they won't hurt their head.

**10** **Listen and stick.** Work with a friend. TR: A7

1     2     3     4     5

| Skateboarding is<br>That trick is<br>Those knee pads look<br>This boy's helmet looks | so<br>very<br>really<br>incredibly<br>extremely | cool.<br>exciting.<br>scary.<br>dangerous.<br>difficult.<br>silly. |
| --- | --- | --- |

**11** **Read and answer.** Look at the pictures. Then complete the sentences.

1. I think that riding a bike _____.

2. In my opinion, skateboarding _____.

3. The cyclist's trick _____.

4. The skateboarder's helmet _____.

5. The boy's bike _____.

It says, 'The equipment is expensive' and 'You fly like a bird'.

I think it's hang-gliding!

**12** **Play a game.** Work in a small group. Choose three sports. Write five sentences about each sport without giving the name of the sport. Exchange your sentences with another group. Guess the sports.

13

# Amazing Adventurers

Danny MacAskill

Danny MacAskill and Bethany Hamilton are two incredibly brave athletes who love being outdoors. Both have known success and failure in their lives.

Danny MacAskill is a skilful cyclist who flips off buildings and rides trains on his bicycle. He has often fallen out of trees and crashed since he began extreme cycling. He's been very lucky – serious accidents often happen to athletes, but he has only broken a few bones and 12 helmets. Every time he's in hospital, he thinks of new places to ride. Born in 1985 in Scotland, he loved cycling as a child, but he never expected to be famous. Then, in 2009, a video of him appeared on YouTube and was watched 27 million times. In 2012, he became a National Geographic 'Adventurer of the Year'.

Super-cool surfer Bethany Hamilton was born in Hawaii in 1990. She was already an extremely skilful surfer at the age of eight. But in 2003, when she was just 13 years old, a shark attacked her and she lost her left arm. Just one month after her injury, she was back in the water. Since then, she has learnt to surf with one arm. She needs more strength in her legs than other surfers because she has only one arm, but she has won competitions. She has written a book about her accident. The book became a film in 2011.

**Risk**

low →→→→→→→→→ high

| skateboarding | BMX | kitesurfing |
| cycling | surfing | extreme cycling |
| skiing | horse riding | heli-skiing |
| hang-gliding | | |

Bethany Hamilton

**14** **Read and write.** Read the text again.
Write **T** for *True* or **F** for *False*.

1. Danny and Bethany both do water sports. _____

2. They both continued to do their sport after they had an injury. _____

3. Bethany was in the water just one year after the shark attacked her. _____

4. Danny and Bethany are both National Geographic Adventurers of the Year. _____

5. They have both known how to do their sport since they were young. _____

**15** **Complete the table.** Write the information.
Compare your answers with a friend.

|  | **Danny MacAskill** | **Bethany Hamilton** |
|---|---|---|
| **When they were born** | | |
| **Where they were born** | | |
| **Sport they participate in** | | |
| **Why they are famous** | | |

**16** **Work with a friend.**
Compare the two athletes in the text. Decide which person is braver, which is cooler and which is luckier. Explain why you think this. Does your friend agree? Why or why not?

More people are killed by drinks machines than by sharks each year.

I think Danny is braver because he performs really dangerous tricks.

But Bethany started surfing one month after her accident. That's incredibly brave!

## Biographical Paragraphs

A biographical paragraph describes the life of another person. When you write a biographical paragraph, you can make it more interesting for the reader if you connect the dates and events in that person's life. Words you can use to link the dates and events include: *after (that), before, since then, the next year, then, at the time, suddenly* and *afterwards*.

**17** **Read.** Read the biography. Underline the expressions that are used to link the events.

## High climber

Before the age of nine, Matt Moniz enjoyed summer holidays like all children do. Then his life suddenly changed. Matt's father invited him to join a climb to Mount Everest. At the time, Matt did not know what to expect, but he said afterwards that the experience was 'the best of his life'. After that, there was no stopping him! The next year, he climbed two of the world's highest mountains: Africa's Kilimanjaro and Russia's Elbrus. Then, at the age of ten, he climbed Argentina's Aconcagua (a height of 6,962 metres.) Since then, Matt has climbed more mountains with his dad. In 2010, Matt became the youngest person in the world to climb the highest point in all fifty states in the USA – in record time. He loves the outdoors and often talks to other children about spending more time outdoors.

**18** **Write.** Write a short biographical paragraph about someone who has an exciting job, does an exciting sport or has travelled to exciting places. Remember to link the events and dates with connecting expressions.

**19** **Work in a small group.** Share your writing.

# NATIONAL GEOGRAPHIC
# Mission

## Connect with our world.

- Work in a small group. Name some extreme sports. Group them as land, water or air activities.

- How do you connect with nature? Write some outdoor activities that you do.

I ride my bike after school.

- Share your ideas with another group. Are they the same or different? Decide which ideas everyone thinks are best.

'If you're a young person and you like walking, climbing trees or exploring, keep doing that. Because this world needs more people that are connected to Earth.'

J. Michael Fay
**Conservationist**
Explorer-in-Residence

Puerto Vallarta, Mexico

## 20 Plan an extreme sports camp.

1. Work in groups. Use the graphic organiser to help you describe your camp.

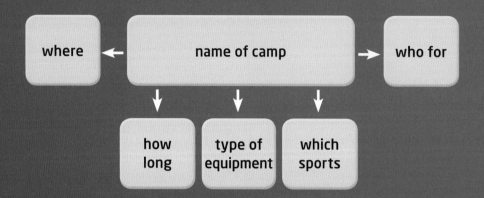

2. Make a brochure or a webpage about the camp.

   a. Write a short summary about the camp. Why is it a great place for visitors or for people to spend their holiday?

   b. Add photos, pictures and a map.

Our summer camp is really fun! You can try all kinds of extreme sports and you'll be near the mountains and the sea!

rts:

parding

rfing

ain Climbing
liding

## Now I can ...

◯ discuss extreme sports.

◯ discuss safety in sports.

◯ describe people and actions.

◯ write a biographical paragraph.

# History's a Mystery

**In this unit, I will ...**
- talk about famous discoveries.
- discuss historical mysteries.
- speculate about the past.
- use examples to support my writing.

**Read and circle the correct answer.**

1. Which of these statements is true?

   a. The Sphinx is in Egypt.

   b. The Sphinx has got the head of a man, but the feet of a cat.

   c. The Sphinx is made from just one piece of stone.

2. The Sphinx was built in 2686 BCE. It is about _____ years old.

   a. 74      b. 2,686      c. 4,700

The Sphinx, Giza, Egypt

**1** **Listen and read.** TR: A10

**2** **Listen and repeat.** TR: A11

Archaeologists have made some incredibly important discoveries – in the desert, in the mountains and under the ground. Discoveries tell us a lot about the past.

**210** BCE

Over 700,000 men built an enormous **tomb** for Chinese **ruler** Qin Shi Huang Di, including this army of terracotta **statues.** When the ruler **died,** the statues were **buried** with him in a tomb. Archaeologists **excavated** the tomb and found over 6,000 statues of soldiers and horses. Each statue is different!

a statue

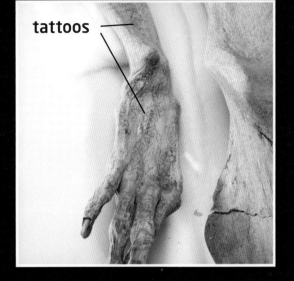

tattoos

**450 CE**
This female **mummy** was found in a tomb in Peru. She was beautifully **preserved**, with **tattoos** of snakes and spiders on her body. No one knows the **cause** of her death or why men were buried with her.

**650 CE**
In 2009, this **treasure** was found in a field in England. Later, archaeologists **discovered** over 3,500 **objects** there. Scientists have **analysed** what they found. They know when the **gold** was buried, but they don't know who buried it or why. Did **thieves** hide it?

treasure

How many statues did they find in China?

More than 6,000.

**3** **Work with a friend.**
What did you learn?
Ask and answer.

# So Much to Learn

*History's a mystery*
*and that's why I like history!*
*Buried statues and mummies, too!*
*So much to learn.*
*So much to do.*

*Excavated kings*
*were found by archaeologists.*
*Anglo-Saxon treasure*
*was discovered*
*in the mist.*

*The Terracotta Army*
*was found deep underground.*
*Just think what you might find*
*if you look around.*

**CHORUS**

*Objects that were hidden*
*can be found by scientists.*
*Pottery and paper,*
*gold and money*
*in the mist.*

*If we learn from history,*
*wisdom from the past*
*can help us answer questions*
*we really want to ask.*

**CHORUS**

**5** **Tick T for *True* or F for *False*.**
Then answer.

1a. The singer thinks history is fun.  Ⓣ Ⓕ

1b. You will be rich if you study history.  Ⓣ Ⓕ

2. Do you like history? Why or why not?

_____

Valley of the Golden Mummies,
near Bawiti, Egypt

25

The Sphinx **was built** around 2500 BCE.
When **were** the statues **discovered**?
The treasure **was discovered** in a field.

It **wasn't excavated** until 1925.
The statues **were found** in 1974.
The objects **weren't stolen**.

**6** **Read.** Complete the sentences. Use the words in brackets.

1. Lots of gold objects _____ (find) in a field by a

   man called Terry Herbert. He had to give the objects to a museum.

2. English treasures _____ (not / find) in a tomb.

   They were found in a field.

3. Four men _____ (bury) with the mummy

   in Peru.

4. Some archaeologists think the Sphinx _____

   (build) around 2500 BCE or earlier. It is made from one stone.

5. The terracotta statues _____ (discover) under

   the ground in the tomb of a Chinese ruler.

terracotta
statues

**7** **What do you know?** Write questions about a famous discovery or a place you know. Work with a friend. Answer each other's questions.

1. _____

2. _____

3. _____

4. _____

5. _____

6. _____

**8** **Work with a friend.** Prepare a role play. Then practise and perform it for the class.

**Student A:**
You are a tourist.
Ask about a discovery
or a place.

**Student B:**
You are a tour guide.
Answer the tourist's
questions.

Excuse me. How many statues were found in the tomb?

Over 6,000 statues were found.

**9** **Listen and repeat.** Then, read and write. TR: A14

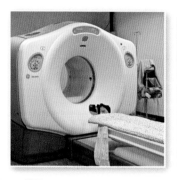
a CT scan

an artefact

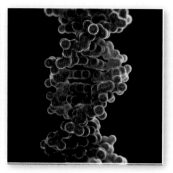
a DNA test

a site

1. Archaeologists can see inside a dead person's body with a _____.

   This test shows if the person had any illnesses and how he or she died.

a sample

2. To learn about a person's family, archaeologists do a _____.

   This test tells them who the person's father was, for example.

3. We can find out what people ate before they died. We can

   take a _____ of food from inside the person's stomach.

4. Archaeologists always study the _____ where something

   was discovered. This helps them to learn why people lived there.

5. Archaeologists often look for pottery and other _____

   near the site. These objects help them learn how people lived.

**10** **Listen and stick.** Order the blue stickers to say what the archaeologist discovered. Then work with a friend. Order the green stickers to say how she solved the mysteries. TR: A15

How did she discover they were from the same family?

I think she did a CT scan!

Are you sure? I don't think so.

1    2    3    4    5

The mummy **was found by hikers**.   The tomb **wasn't found by an archaeologist**.
The bottles **were found by divers**.   The bodies **weren't analysed by scientists**.
**Was** the pottery broken **by thieves**?   **Who was** the treasure **hidden by**?

**11** **Read and answer.** Complete the sentences. Then listen to check your answers. TR: A17

In 1991, a mummy _____was discovered by_____ (discover) hikers

in the mountains. The mummy was over 5,000 years old, but he

_____ (preserve) ice. No one knows his name, so he

_____ (describe) people around the world as the 'Iceman'.

For the next ten years, the Iceman's body _____ (analyse)

scientists. At first, people didn't know how the Iceman died, but in 2001, the

Iceman _____ (study) Paul Gostner, who found an injury

in the Iceman's arm. In 2005, the Iceman _____ (check)

doctors using a new CT scan machine. We now know that he died from the

injury. But who _____ (the Iceman / kill)?

**12** **Play a game.** Play with a friend. Make correct sentences to mark your X or O.

| | | |
|---|---|---|
| the Sphinx<br>analyse<br>archaeologists<br>for 37 years | the Iceman<br>find<br>hikers<br>1991 | gold objects<br>discover<br>Terry Herbert<br>England |
| the terracotta statues<br>make<br>700,000 men<br>China | the Sphinx<br>not<br>excavate<br>until 1925 | a mummy<br>find<br>tomb<br>Peru |
| English treasure<br>hide<br>a field<br>650 BCE | the Sphinx<br>build<br>Egyptians<br>around 2686 BCE | the Iceman's injury<br>analyse<br>doctors<br>2005 |

29

# The Amazing Discovery of King Tut

Egypt is full of really exciting and ancient discoveries, but the most famous is the tomb of King Tutankhamun (King Tut). Howard Carter and another English archaeologist spent years looking for the tomb. In 1922, Carter found it, after someone discovered an artefact with the king's name on it near the site. Inside the tomb, Carter found hundreds of gold objects, more than 3,000 treasures and – most importantly – King Tut's mummy. Although King Tut was buried over 3,000 years ago, his DNA was perfectly preserved. Later, Dr Zahi Hawass, a famous Egyptian archaeologist, moved the artefacts and the mummy to a museum.

Who was King Tut? He was an Egyptian boy who became a ruler in 1333 BCE – at the age of nine. We know from the date of some artefacts that he ruled until he died in 1323 BCE. Tut was buried with all the objects he would need in his next life. Why did he die so young? The cause of his death is not known. In 1968, his mummy was analysed by scientists who found broken bones in Tut's skull. A CT scan of Tut's mummy in 2006 showed that he broke his leg before he died. A DNA test showed that he had malaria. No one knows how he died. History's a mystery!

## 14 Read and write. Answer the questions.

1. How did Carter know where to find King Tut's tomb?

_____

2. Why was King Tut buried with so many objects?

_____

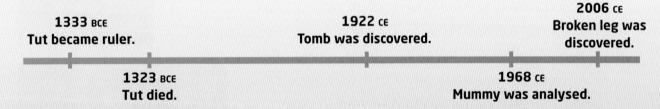

weird but true

Mummy brown was a paint colour made from ground-up mummies. It was used during the 16th and 17th centuries.

3. How many years was King Tut the ruler?

_____

4. What are two possible causes of King Tut's death?

_____

## 15 Look at the timeline. Write complete sentences about each date.

**1333 BCE**
Tut became ruler.

**1922 CE**
Tomb was discovered.

**2006 CE**
Broken leg was discovered.

**1323 BCE**
Tut died.

**1968 CE**
Mummy was analysed.

## 16 Work with a friend. Choose a paragraph to talk about. Your friend will listen and make notes. Then listen to your friend talk about the other paragraph. Make notes.

| | |
|---|---|
| Howard Carter | |
| The discovery of King Tut's tomb | |
| King Tut | |
| Analysing King Tut's mummy | |

## Paragraphs of Exemplification

In a paragraph of exemplification, you give examples that support important ideas in your text. Be clear and show the reader that you know what you are writing about. To do this, add examples of facts. Use expressions like: *for instance*, *such as*, *namely*, *specifically* and *a good example is*. These words let the reader know that more information is coming in the text.

**17** **Read.** Underline all the expressions that refer to examples.

## Memories from the past

Archaeologists feel very excited when new discoveries are made because each new discovery tells them more about the past. A good example is the famous Iceman mummy discovered in 1991 by hikers in the Alps. Thanks to DNA tests, CT scans and artefacts found near the site, we know more about people who lived long ago, namely, what they wore and how they lived. The Iceman tells us a lot. So does the famous Peruvian female mummy. For instance, we know that women were given tattoos. We also know from the mummy's tomb that men were buried together with important women (before she was excavated, we thought that only women were buried with important men). Although we still don't know everything about these mummies (specifically, the cause of their death), the Iceman and the Peruvian mummy are two incredible discoveries that tell us more about the past.

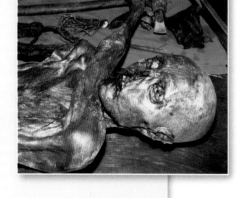

**18** **Write.** Write about the terracotta statues and King Tut's tomb. What do these two discoveries tell us about the past? Use examples from both.

**19** **Work in a small group.** Share your writing.

# Mission

## Learn about local history.

- Work in a group. Is it important to protect historical places in your country? Why or why not? Discuss.

- Which places are of historical interest in your area? Who can you talk to in order to find out more information? Discuss and write the best ideas in the box.

'*I decided that I wanted to learn more about civilisations of the past and about people living totally different lives from mine. I could not believe my luck when I found there was an actual profession for this type of work – anthropology.*'

**Johan Reinhard**
Anthropologist
Explorer-in-Residence

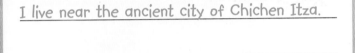

I live near the ancient city of Chichen Itza.

- Work with another group. Share your ideas. Are they the same or different? Which idea does everyone like best?

Johan Reinhard on the summit
of Nevado Ampato, Peru

## 20 Research a mystery.

1. Choose a mystery that you are interested in.

2. Find pictures and information to use in a poster.

3. Include a brief report as part of your poster presentation.

Some people think these mysterious lines were made by ancient tribes.

The Nasca lines are very big drawings in the South of Peru. The Nasca people lived there 2,000 years ago. The lines were discovered in the 1920s. The drawings show huge animals, people, shapes and lines.

# Unit 3
# Chocolate!

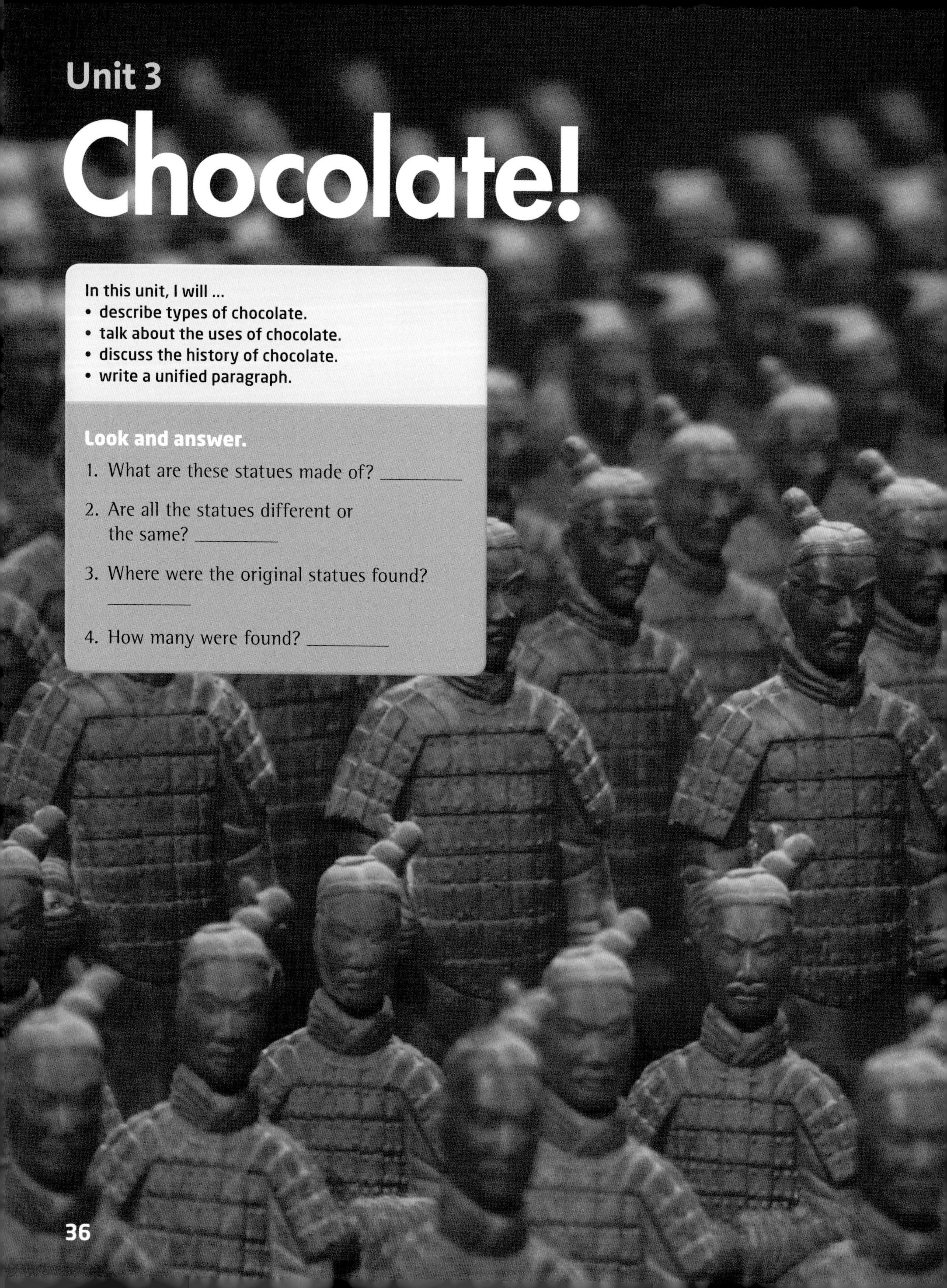

**In this unit, I will ...**
- describe types of chocolate.
- talk about the uses of chocolate.
- discuss the history of chocolate.
- write a unified paragraph.

**Look and answer.**

1. What are these statues made of? _____

2. Are all the statues different or the same? _____

3. Where were the original statues found? _____

4. How many were found? _____

**World Chocolate Wonderland exhibition, Taipei**

**1** **Listen and read.** TR: A19

**2** **Listen and repeat.** TR: A20

One thousand years ago, chocolate was so valuable that it was used as money! Now we use chocolate every day and on special **occasions**, such as International Chocolate Day on 13ᵗʰ September.

Chocolate comes from the cacao tree that grows near the equator. After four years, the trees start to produce **pods**. Farmers open the pods and take out the seeds. **Vanilla**, sugar, **cinnamon** and other **spices** are added to the ground-up seeds.

The **origin** of chocolate is interesting. As early as 2,000 years ago, people of the Americas were mixing cacao beans, water and spices to make a drink. In 1502, Christopher Columbus brought cacao beans back to Spain. People later learnt how to change chocolate from **liquid** to **solid**. And by 1847 they were enjoying chocolate **bars**!

Today there are about 40,000 **types** of **chocolate bars**. We have milk and dark chocolate in fun shapes, some with delicious **fillings** like **caramel**. We have **hot chocolate**, chocolate ice cream, cereal, biscuits, **milkshakes**, cocoa **powder** and even chocolate sculptures!

pods

vanilla

cinnamon

spices

powder

solid

liquid

caramel

a hot chocolate

a milkshake

**3** **Work with a friend.** What did you learn?
Ask and answer.

How many types of chocolate bars are there?

Thousands!

## 4 Listen, read and sing. TR: A21

# Hot Chocolate

*Tell me! Do you like hot chocolate?*

**Put some chocolate in a cup.**
**Get some milk and heat it up.**
**Stir in some vanilla. Add some spice.**
**Sprinkle on some cinnamon.**

*It'll taste nice!*

*I was making hot chocolate*
*in the kitchen one night.*
*My grandmother was telling me*
*I wasn't doing it right.*

*She was telling me about her mother,*
*about how she made cocoa when she was young.*
*She was telling me to sit down*
*when she said, 'I'm going to show you how it's done.'*

*CHORUS*

*Hot chocolate in a cup.*
*Hot chocolate! Pour it to the top.*
*Hot chocolate tastes so nice.*
*I learnt to make it like Grandmother said I should!*

*I love hot chocolate!*

*CHORUS*

*Hot chocolate in a cup.*
*Hot chocolate! Pour it to the top.*
*Hot chocolate tastes so nice.*
*I learnt to make it like Grandmother said I should!*

*Hot chocolate!*

## 5 Answer the questions.

1. Who taught the singer how to make hot chocolate?

   _____

2. Circle five ingredients she puts in it.

3. Do you know how to make hot chocolate?

## GRAMMAR TR: A22

By 250 CE, people **were drinking** hot chocolate.
We **were** still **talking** about chocolate **when** the bell rang.
**Was** the cacao tree **growing** in Africa by then?
No, it wasn't. But it **was growing** in Africa by the late 1800s.

**6** **Read.** What were the people in the photos doing on International Chocolate Day? Use these phrases.

| | | |
|---|---|---|
| paint a picture | design a poster | present a report |
| make a milkshake | do research | eat chocolate bars |

**7** **Write.** What were you doing yesterday? Write true sentences.

1. At 7 a.m. <u>I was getting the bus to school</u>                .

2. At 9 a.m. _____ .

3. At lunchtime _____

   when _____ .

4. At 4.30 p.m. _____ .

5. At 7 p.m. _____

   when _____ .

6. At 8.30 p.m. _____ .

7. At 10 p.m. _____

   when _____ .

**8** **Work in a group.** Guess what everyone was doing yesterday. Take turns.

Were you doing homework at 7 p.m.?

Yes, I was.

43

**9** **Listen and repeat.** Then, read and write. TR: A23

a gram

mix

pour

a recipe

ingredients

a teaspoon

1. Learn how to make a delicious chocolate milkshake with this

   _____recipe_____!

2. First, make sure you've got all the _____: vanilla ice cream, milk,

   cocoa powder and little pieces of dark chocolate.

3. Put 2 scoops of vanilla ice cream, 1 cup of milk and 6 _____ of

   cocoa powder into a blender. _____ the ingredients well.

4. When the liquid is ready, _____ the milkshake into two glasses.

   Decorate them with 30 _____ of dark chocolate. Enjoy!

**10** **Work with a friend.** Stick the recipe in the correct order.
Then listen to check your answers. TR: A24

> I think 'find the ingredients' is the first step.

> I agree.

1    2    3    4    5

| CAUSE | EFFECT |
|---|---|
| The boy **printed** out the recipe | **so that** he **could read** it whilst he was cooking. |
| We **put** all the ingredients on the table | **so that** it **would be** easier to find them later. |

**11** **Read and write.** Connect the cause and the effect.

1. Joseph Fry added new ingredients ... (→ make a solid chocolate bar.)

_so that he could make a solid chocolate bar_ .

2. Sugar was mixed with chocolate ... (→ taste sweeter.)

_____ .

3. Chocolate companies put caramel in chocolate ... (→ have more variety.)

_____ .

4. An American company printed a recipe ... (→ people make chocolate at home.)

_____ .

5. Chocolate was ground and heated ... (→ be smooth and melt.)

_____ .

**12** **Play a game.** Cut out the cards on page 161. Play with a friend.
Ask and answer. Take turns.

# The Story of Chocolate

The story of chocolate starts with the Olmecs and the Mayan people who lived in the Americas more than 1,000 years ago. The Mayas have been growing cacao trees and using the seeds to make chocolate drinks for 2,000 years or more. In fact, scientists have analysed chocolate residue from a ceramic 'teapot'. The results suggest that the Mayas were drinking chocolate as early as 2,600 years ago! Some artefacts show people pouring the liquid into cups. The Mayas also used the seeds as currency. With ten seeds they could buy a rabbit in the market.

The story continues with the Aztecs, who also loved chocolate and prepared it hot like the Mayas. But the Aztecs added spices so that it would taste better. Some rich people drank chocolate for breakfast, lunch and dinner. Some were even buried with chocolate so that they could take it with them to the next world. Between 1200 and 1500 CE, the Aztecs also used chocolate as currency. In fact, by 1500, people were paying 30 seeds for a rabbit.

Let's continue our journey! When the Spanish arrived in the Aztec capital in 1519 CE, they tried chocolate and hated it. Without sugar it was extremely bitter, so the Spanish mixed it with sugar. In 1528 CE, the Spanish took the Aztec seeds and recipe back to Spain so that they could drink chocolate there. Before this, no one in Europe knew about chocolate!

**Weird but true**

People say that the Aztec ruler Moctezuma II drank 50 cups of chocolate a day.

**14** **Complete the chart.** Write the cause or effect of each action.

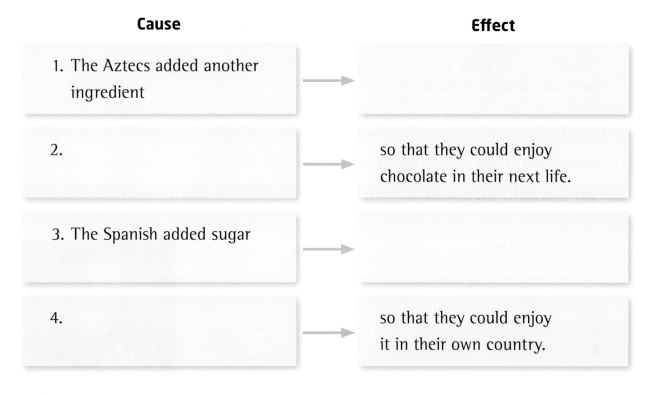

| Cause | Effect |
|---|---|
| 1. The Aztecs added another ingredient | |
| 2. | so that they could enjoy chocolate in their next life. |
| 3. The Spanish added sugar | |
| 4. | so that they could enjoy it in their own country. |

**15** **Read the text again.** Write how chocolate changed over time in these ways.

1. People: _The Olmecs and the Mayas used it, first._

_Then the Aztecs used it. Finally, the Spanish began to use chocolate._

2. Ingredients: _____

3. Chocolate as currency: _____

**16** **Work in a group of three.** Retell the story of chocolate. Take turns.

Temple of the Great Jaguar,
Tikal, Guatemala

## Paragraph Unity

A good paragraph has unity – all the sentences in the paragraph refer to and explain the main idea. The topic sentence expresses the main idea and the supporting sentences give related details that extend the main idea. When you write your paragraph, check to make sure all the sentences are closely related to the topic.

**17** **Read.** There are three sentences in each blog response that do not belong. Find and cross out the sentences.

### Chocolate customs

Keiko, Osaka  In my country, Japan, chocolate is important in some celebrations. The origin of chocolate is interesting. My favourite celebration is Valentine's Day in February, when women usually give chocolate to men to show their appreciation or love. International Chocolate Day is in September. One month later, on 14th March – or 'White Day' – men give chocolate to women. In South Korea people celebrate Valentine's Day with chocolate, too. South Korea is about 700 miles away from Japan.

Pablo, Mexico City  In my family we use chocolate on 'Day of the Dead', a Mexican holiday that takes place in early November. The capital of Mexico is Mexico City. This is a time when we remember our friends and family who have died. Today there are more than 40,000 types of chocolate bars. My family uses chocolate in two ways. First, my mum cooks a meal with chocolate sauce. (It's her own recipe, and it's delicious!) Then, we buy skulls that are made of milk or dark chocolate. I don't like chocolate milkshakes.

**18** **Write.** Write about a custom in your family or a special occasion when people use chocolate. Make sure all the sentences are closely related to the topic.

**19** **Work in a small group.** Share your writing.

# NATIONAL GEOGRAPHIC
# Mission

## Learn about your food.

- Why is it important to learn about the ingredients in your food?

- Find some chocolate wrappers and look at the labels. What can you learn about the chocolate from these labels? Work in a small group. Think of ideas. Talk about and write the best ones in the box.

'We all have a chance to save the Earth, through our fork, through our plates.'

Barton Seaver
Chef/Conservationist
National Geographic Fellow

> Some chocolate bars have more cocoa in
>
> them than others.

- Work with another group. Share your ideas. Are they the same or different? Which ideas does everyone like best?

49

## 20 Make a collection of chocolate recipes.

1. Research recipes that include chocolate.

2. Choose one that you like and bring the recipe to class. (If possible, try the recipe at home first!)

3. Work in small groups. Make a collection of chocolate recipes.

   a. Write the recipes in your own words on cards.

   b. Add photos and pictures.

   c. Pin the recipe cards together.

Chocolate Ice Cream Bread

Ingredients:
2 cups melted
    chocolate ice cream
1½ cups self-raising flour
Put the flour in the bowl.
Pour in the melted ice cream.
. the ingredients well.
ur into a greased tin.
ake for 35-40 minutes at
    350°F (175°C)
Let it cool.
Enjoy!

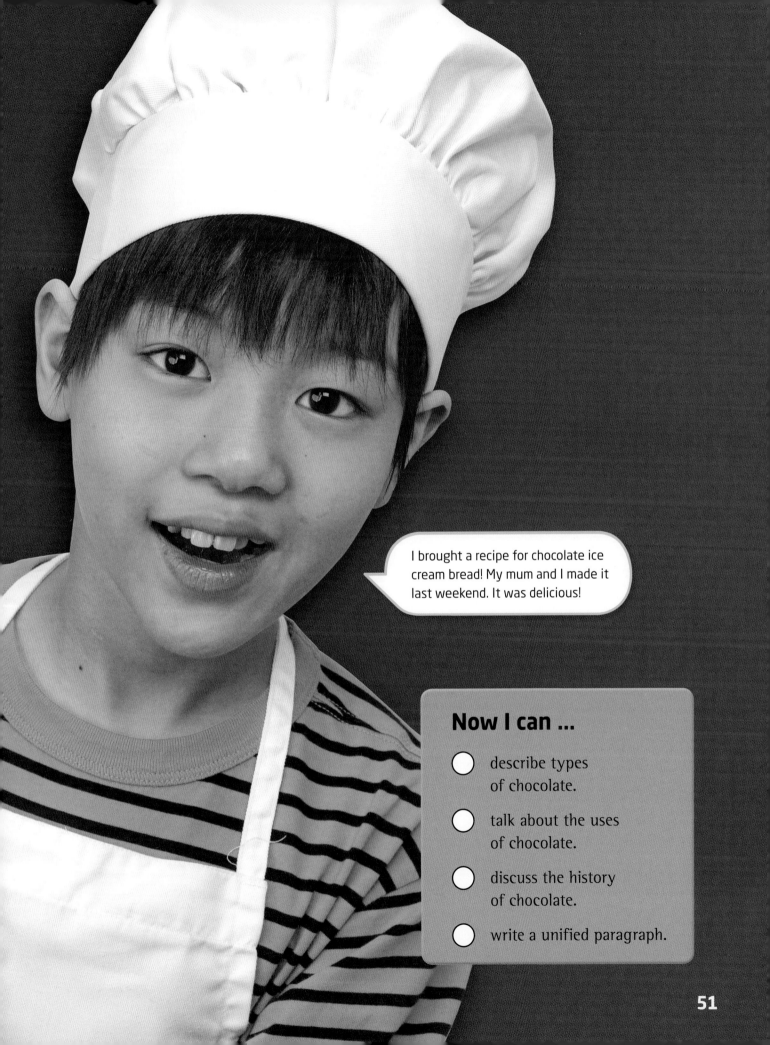

I brought a recipe for chocolate ice cream bread! My mum and I made it last weekend. It was delicious!

## Now I can ...

- ○ describe types of chocolate.
- ○ talk about the uses of chocolate.
- ○ discuss the history of chocolate.
- ○ write a unified paragraph.

# Review

**1** **Listen to the phone call.** Tick the things that Carlos has done. TR: A27

    ◯ learnt to surf      ◯ fallen in the water a lot      ◯ surfed skilfully

    ◯ worn a life jacket      ◯ had an accident      ◯ been hang-gliding

**2** **Listen again.** Answer the questions. TR: A28

1. How long has Carlos been at the campsite? _____ _for four days_ _____

2. How many times has he fallen in the water? _____

3. Is it raining today? _____

4. How many years has the teacher done extreme sports? _____

5. Why did he have to wear a life jacket and helmet yesterday? _____

_____

6. Why did his friend show him how to climb rocks? _____

_____

**3** **Work with a friend.** Discuss a holiday or camping trip that you enjoyed. Ask and answer questions. Use the words in the box.

| | |
|---|---|
| extremely | weather |
| incredibly | city or country |
| really | activities |
| so | place where you stayed |
| very | family |
| absolutely | friends |

I went on a hiking holiday in the mountains once. It was absolutely brilliant!

Really? What was the weather like?

**4** **Look at the pictures.** What were the boys and their sister doing at these times? Draw lines.

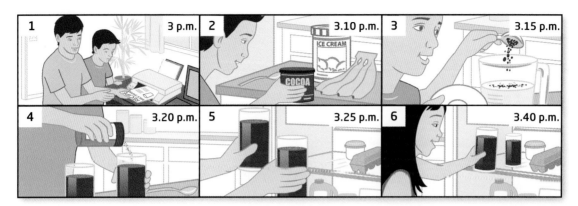

1. At 3 p.m.
2. At 3.10 p.m.
3. At 3.15 p.m.
4. At 3.20 p.m.
5. At 3.25 p.m.
6. At 3.40 p.m.

a. Alex was putting the ingredients on the table.
b. they were putting the milkshakes in the fridge because they were planning to drink them after their football match.
c. the boys' sister was taking their milkshakes!
d. Daniel was printing the recipe.
e. the boys were putting cocoa powder into the blender.
f. they were pouring the liquid into glasses and putting cinnamon on top.

**5** **Work with a friend.** Look at the pictures. Tell the story. Add details.

**6** **Work with a friend.** Ask and answer questions. Make notes.

1. Where / the Sphinx / build? _____ Where was the Sphinx built? _____

2. When / the terracotta statues / make? _____

3. Where / the ruler Tutankhamun / buried? _____

4. Who / the first solid bar of chocolate / invent / by? _____

5. Tutankhamun's treasures / excavate / by / archaeologists? _____

_____

6. surfing / invent / in Hawaii? _____

**7** **Listen to the answers.** Win a point for each correct answer! TR: A29

53

# Let's Talk

## I love it!

I will ...
- start a conversation.
- change the topic.
- bring the topic back on track.
- discuss likes and dislikes.

**1** **Listen and read.** TR: A30

Leo:    Hey, **is everyone ready** for the camping trip?

Andy:   Yes, I packed my rucksack this morning.

Carl:   **By the way,** have you seen that new shark film yet?

Andy:   No, I haven't. **What's it like?**

Carl:   It's amazing. **I love it.**

Leo:    I do, too. **Anyway,** let's talk about it later. **Back to** camping. Has anyone got a sleeping bag I can borrow?

| Is everyone ready?<br>Ready?<br>Let's start. | By the way, ...<br>Hey!<br>Before I forget, ... | What's it like?<br>What's it about?<br>Is it good? | Anyway, ...<br>Back to ...<br>Look, ... |
|---|---|---|---|
| | | I like it. / I love it.<br>I hate it. / I can't stand it. | |

**2** **Work in groups of three.** Have a conversation. Use the expressions in the table. Take turns. Change the subject to something else.

# Excuse me, please.

I will ...
- ask for clarification.
- express doubt.
- interrupt politely.

**3** **Listen and read.** TR: A31

| | |
|---|---|
| Karen: | **What did she say**? |
| Emma: | **I think she said** we have to match the pictures and sentences, **but I'm not sure**. |
| Nadia: | **I missed it, too.** Let's ask her. |
| Nadia: | **Excuse me**, Miss Turner. **Could you repeat that, please**? |
| Miss Turner: | **Yes. I'll go over it again**. |

| **What did** _____ **say?** I didn't catch that. I missed that. | **I think she said** _____ **, but I'm not sure.** I'm not sure. **I missed it, too.** Let's check. | **Excuse me** _____ . I'm sorry, _____ . Could I ask a question, please? | **Could you repeat that, please?** Could you say / explain that again? | **Yes.** No problem! Of course! |
|---|---|---|---|---|
| | | | | **I'll go over it again.** I'll explain it again. |

**4** **Listen.** You will hear two discussions. (Circle) the answers. TR: A32

1. What do the students think the teacher told them to do?
   a. practise a dialogue    b. write a dialogue    c. listen to a dialogue

2. Who didn't hear what the teacher said?
   a. the boy    b. the girl    c. the boy and the girl

**5** **Work in groups of three.** Choose a situation and discuss.

1. Your teacher is telling you about a survey you are going to do. You didn't catch all the instructions.

2. Your teacher is going over the answers. You missed the last answer.

3. Your teacher is explaining tonight's homework. You didn't quite understand it.

# Water, Water Everywhere

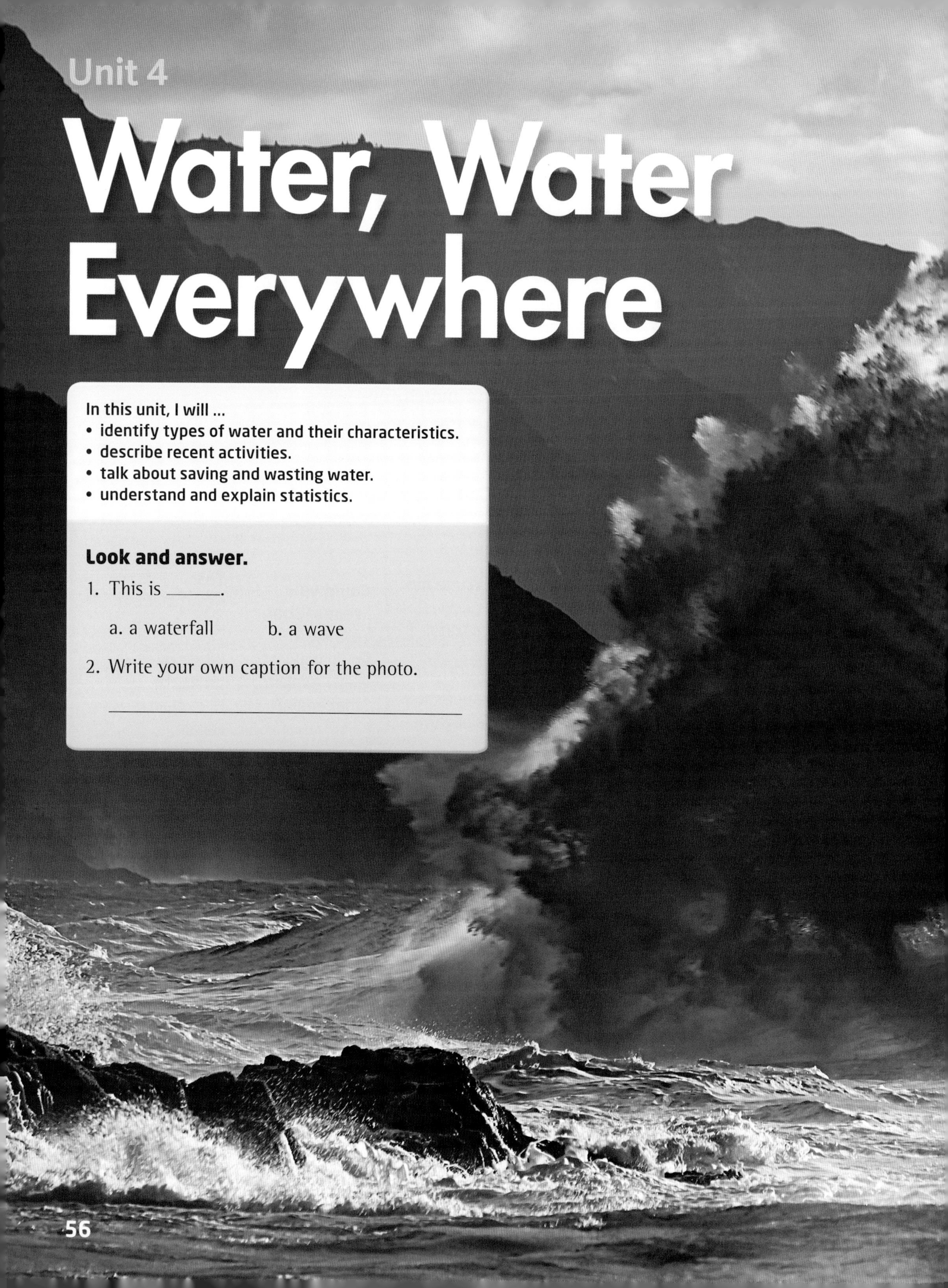

**In this unit, I will ...**
- identify types of water and their characteristics.
- describe recent activities.
- talk about saving and wasting water.
- understand and explain statistics.

**Look and answer.**

1. This is _____.

   a. a waterfall          b. a wave

2. Write your own caption for the photo.

   _____

Na Pali Coast, Kauai, Hawaii

Some of the most beautiful places on Earth are made up of water: oceans, seas, rivers, **waterfalls** and ice. Read about three famous **wet** places.

Do you like **soaking** your feet in the sea? The **salt water** in the Dead Sea is good for your body. This sea is about eight times saltier than an ocean. You can **float** on it. It is about 400 metres (1,312 feet) below **sea level** and is the world's deepest **saltwater lake**.

The beautiful Hubbard **Glacier** has been flowing slowly towards the ocean for centuries, **carving** rocks along the way. It is formed from **drops of water** that **froze** billions of years ago. Around 70 per cent of **fresh water** on the planet's surface is frozen.

a glacier

a swamp

The Asmat **Swamp** is home to amazing animals like crocodiles, sea snakes and Komodo dragons. These wetlands are important because they provide a home to many creatures and they control floods. Also, the plants **filter** dirty water and make it clean.

**3** **Work with a friend.** What did you learn? Ask and answer.

Is the Dead Sea below sea level?

Yes, it is. It's about 400 metres below sea level.

**4** **Listen, read and sing.** TR: A35

# A World of Water

*A world of wonder. A world of water.*
*I've been thinking about*
*all the water in our world.*

*CHORUS*

*There's water in lakes and water in the sea.*
*There's even water in you and me!*

*A puddle of water. A waterfall.*
*A tall glass of water. I love it all!*

*Fresh water, salt water, water in the sink.*
*I've been taking some time to think*
*about how much water there is in the world!*
*It's everywhere!*

*CHORUS*

*Fresh water, salt water, water in the sink.*
*I've been taking more time to think.*
*Why do we need water in this world?*

*We need water for crops and water for grass.*
*We need water for plants and animals, too!*

*Everything needs water.*
*Everything needs water.*
*I know that's true!*

*CHORUS*

*A world of wonder. A world of water.*
*Have you been thinking about*
*all the water in our world?*

**5** **Answer the questions.**

1. Circle four things that need water.

2. Is there water inside you?   Yes   No

3. Invent a new title for the song!

_____

Iguazu Falls, on the border
of Argentina and Brazil

How long **have** you and your sister **been having** swimming lessons?

I**'ve been having** swimming lessons **for** three months.
                                    **for** about a year.
My sister **has been having** swimming lessons **since** March.
                                    **since** she was nine.

**6** **Read and write.** Complete the sentences.

| play | soak | surf | have | water |

1. It _____has been raining_____ since three o'clock. It's really wet

   outside now.

2. My brother _____ water polo for three years.

3. I _____ in the bath for half an hour. It feels

   so nice!

4. Mum and Dad _____ the plants in the garden for

   15 minutes.

5. My sister _____ a shower for nearly 30 minutes.

   She spends ages in the shower!

6. You're a good surfer. How long _____ you

   _____?

**7** **What about you?** Imagine you are visiting three of these places. On a sheet of paper, write at least *three* things that you have been doing at each place. Don't say the name of the place!

> The Dead Sea
>
> The Asmat Swamp
>
> The Hubbard Glacier
>
> The Pyramids
>
> Qin Shi Huang Di's tomb

I've been counting statues.

**8** **Work in a group.** Listen to each other's sentences. Guess where people are. Take turns.

I've been feeling very cold today.

No, I'm not. Try again. Here's another clue.

Are you in the Dead Sea?

**9** **Listen and repeat.** Look at the pictures. Complete the sentences. TR: A37

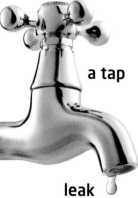

a tap

leak

a drain

save

running
water

waste

1. There are many ways you can _____ water at home.

   For example, you can have a shower instead of a bath. Showers use less water.

2. If the dishwasher isn't full when you use it, you'll _____ water.

3. Use the handle to turn off the _____ while you brush your

   teeth. Turn it on again when you need it.

4. Taps that _____ waste a lot of fresh water. If you see drops of

   water coming from a tap, tell someone.

5. Don't throw rubbish down the _____.

6. When we went camping, we didn't have _____.

**10** **Listen and stick.** Work with a friend. Compare your answers. TR: A38

> If you leave the water running, you waste 11 litres per minute!

> That's right! We should turn off the tap when we brush our teeth.

| (11) litres | (15) litres | (40) litres | (75) litres | (230) litres | (265) litres |

Do **whatever** you can to save water.
Save fresh water **whenever** you can and **wherever** you go.
**Whoever** threw paint down the drain is in trouble!

**11** **Read.** Complete the sentences.

1. _____ people throw rubbish down a drain, they

    pollute water.

2. _____ told the teacher about that leaking tap,

    saved water.

3. People use 265 litres of water _____ they have

    a bath.

4. _____ glaciers are found, the average yearly

    temperature is below freezing.

5. _____ you leave the tap running while you brush

    your teeth, you waste 11 litres of water every minute.

6. People should do _____ they can to protect

    the sea.

**12** **Play a game.** Cut out the board game on page 163. Play the
game in a small group.

Whenever I have a shower,
I save water.

That's great! Now it's
my turn!

# A World of Water

Nearly 75 per cent of the Earth is covered by water. There is water above ground called *surface water*, such as lakes, swamps and rivers, and water that's under the ground called *groundwater*. Water even exists in the sky! That is called *water vapour*. There is water everywhere.

Although we have a lot of water, we can't drink most of it. 97.5 per cent of the earth's water is salt water, which humans can't drink. The rest is fresh water, which we can drink. However, we can't use most of our drinking water because 70 per cent is frozen – like the Hubbard Glacier. Also, we can only reach 30 per cent of our groundwater and most of that is polluted. In fact, we can only drink about one per cent of the world's fresh water.

We don't drink most of our fresh water. Only five per cent goes to the taps in our homes. About 95 per cent is used to produce food, clothes and energy. We don't see that water, but it is a big part of our 'water footprint', or the total amount of water we use. For example, we don't see the water that was used to make a T-shirt. We only see the T-shirt. But 2,700 litres (713 gallons) of water were used to produce it!

Earth has always had the same amount of water. However, there are more people on the planet now and we all need water. If we want water in the future, we must not waste it or pollute it now!

**Three litres of water are used to produce a one-litre bottle of water.**

### The World's Water Resources

**75%**
of the Earth is covered in water

**97.5%**
of that is ocean

which leaves **2.5%**
as fresh water

**70%**
of that is ice

which leaves **30%**
as groundwater we can get access to

Much of that is so polluted it's unuseable leaving less than **1%** of the world's fresh water (or about 0.007% of all water on earth) readily accessible for direct human use.

Iguazu Falls

## 14 Read. Complete the definitions.

1. Water in lakes, rivers and swamps is called _____.

2. Water in the clouds or sky is referred to as _____.

3. Water that is underground is called _____.

4. The water we can drink is called _____.

## 15 Read. Label the graphs.

**Where does our fresh water go?**

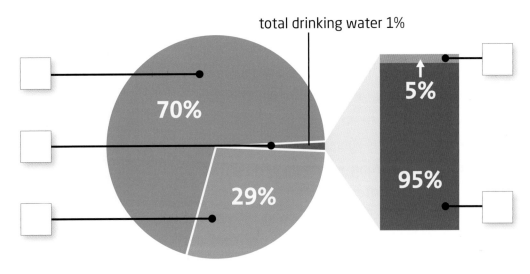

1. To our homes
2. Frozen
3. To produce food, clothes and energy
4. Polluted groundwater
5. In clean places that we can reach

## 16 Work with a friend. Discuss the information in the graphs.

There is a lot of fresh water on our planet.

But we can't use 70 per cent of it because it's frozen.

## Paragraphs of Information

When you write a paragraph of information, you should state facts and statistics and give examples.

**17** **Read.** Read the paragraph of information. Underline the statistics.

## Save water outdoors!

About five per cent of the world's fresh water goes to our homes for drinking, cooking and cleaning. The average family uses one quarter of their fresh water in the garden! In many countries, people waste 50 to 80 per cent of their garden water because they water grass when it's hot outside! People should water early in the morning or late in the afternoon when there is less sun. People also waste 10 to 35 litres of water every time they leave a hose running for one minute. But why do we use our drinking water on grass? We could collect rainwater to water the plants!

People wash their cars with our drinking water, too! When people wash their cars at home, 50 per cent of the chemicals from car soap goes down the drain and flows into freshwater rivers. Today, about 40 per cent of our rivers are polluted. Remind your family and friends where the water goes. You can make a difference!

**18** **Write.** Write a paragraph of information. Describe ways to save water inside your home. Give examples. Remember to include facts and statistics.

**19** **Work in a small group.** Share your ideas.

# NATIONAL GEOGRAPHIC
# Mission

## Conserve water at school.

'I just want to do my part to be sure we humans conserve water and share it with all of life.'

Sandra Postel
**Fresh Water Conservationist**
National Geographic Fellow

- Work in a small group. Discuss how water is used in your school every day, such as in the classrooms, canteen, outside and at sports facilities. Where do you think most water is used?

- How can you help save water in your school? Think of ideas. Discuss and write the best ideas below.

We can use rainwater to water the plants.

_____

_____

_____

_____

- Work with another group. Share your ideas. Are they the same or different? Which ideas does everyone like best?

## 20  Make a world map of water.

1. Work in groups of three.

2. Research two bodies of water in the world, such as rivers, lakes or oceans. You can include waterfalls.

3. Write a short summary about each body of water.

4. Print or find a world map. Stick each summary at the location of the body of water.

5. Add photos and pictures to your map.

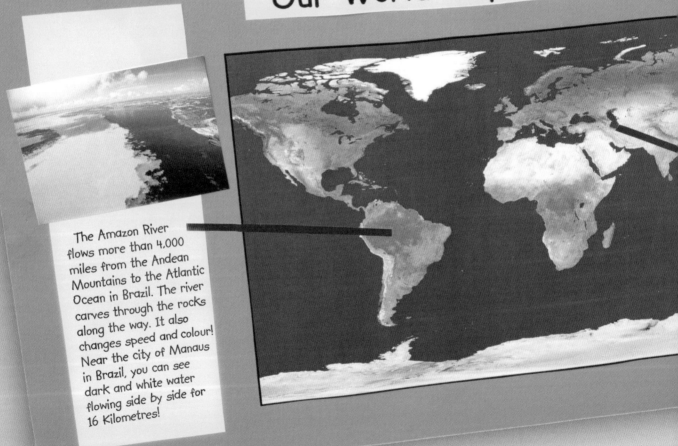

Our World Map of Water

The Amazon River flows more than 4,000 miles from the Andean Mountains to the Atlantic Ocean in Brazil. The river carves through the rocks along the way. It also changes speed and colour! Near the city of Manaus in Brazil, you can see dark and white water flowing side by side for 16 Kilometres!

The Caspian Sea is the largest lake in the world.

The Caspian Sea is the largest lake in the world. It is a saltwater lake. It is 380 thousand square Kilometres. 130 rivers flow into the Caspian Sea. It is bordered by Russia, Azerbaijan, Turkmenistan, Iran and Kazakhstan. It is the only saltwater lake that has seals. Caspian Seals are very sweet!

## Now I can ...

○ identify types of water and their characteristics.

○ describe recent activities.

○ talk about saving and wasting water.

○ understand and explain statistics.

# Unit 5

# It's a Small World

In this unit, I will ...
- identify small creatures and their characteristics.
- describe creatures.
- report what other people say.
- write a science report.

**Look and talk.**

1. Describe this creature in one word.

2. Where does this creature live?

3. What do you think it is?

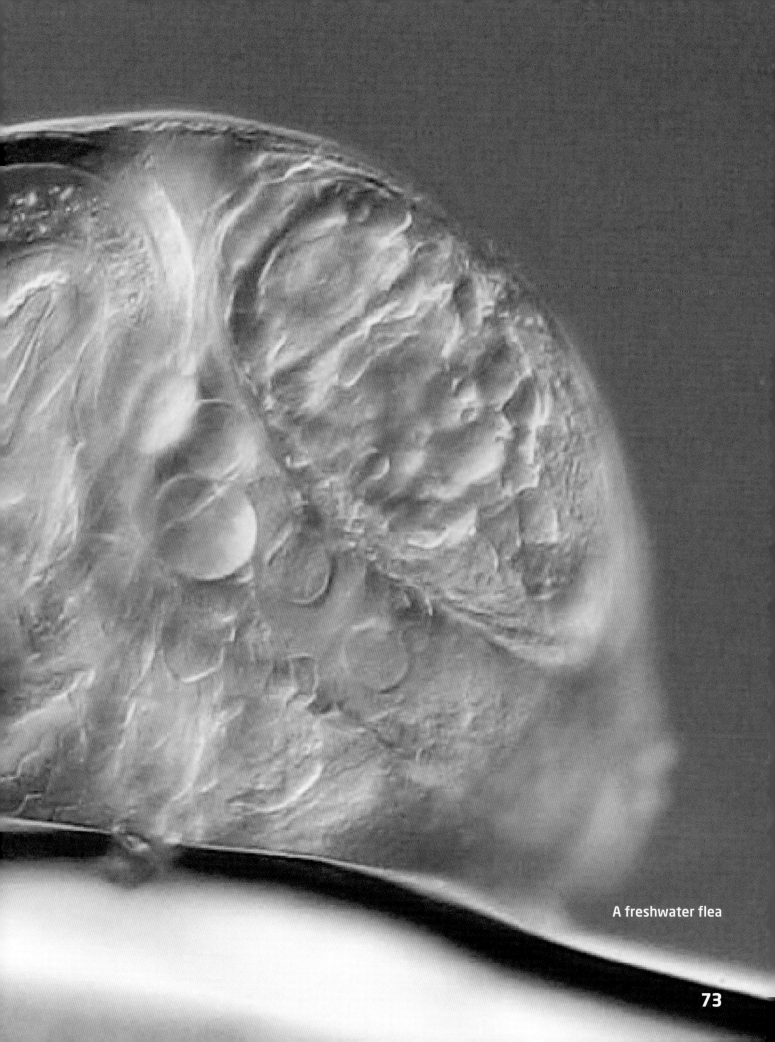

A freshwater flea

## 1 Listen and read. TR: A41

## 2 Listen and repeat. TR: A42

We share our planet with millions of small creatures: cool spiders, beautiful striped butterflies, ugly bugs, cute hamsters and fascinating fish. Can you think of any more little creatures that live on Earth?

Eyelash mites are 0.3 millimetres long. You can only see them through a **microscope**. They look **horrible**, but they're very **common**.

**Habitat**: our eyelashes

Characteristics: These **organisms** eat dead skin **cells**. They crawl around our skin at night.

This sea horse is an orange fish that's just 16 **millimetres** long. It's smaller than a **human's** tooth and has a long **thin** tail.

Habitat: warm water, near coral

Characteristics: It uses camouflage. It **grabs** food that floats by. Male sea horses have babies.

The **male** bee hummingbird is the smallest bird in the world. (It's about five and a half **centimetres** long.) The **female** is bigger. Its eggs are smaller than coffee beans.

Habitat: near flowers

Characteristics: It can move its strong wings 80 times a second.

**3** **Work with a friend.** What did you learn? Ask and answer.

How big is the bee hummingbird?

The male is five and a half centimetres long. The female is bigger.

**Listen, read and sing.** TR: A43

# Look into a Microscope

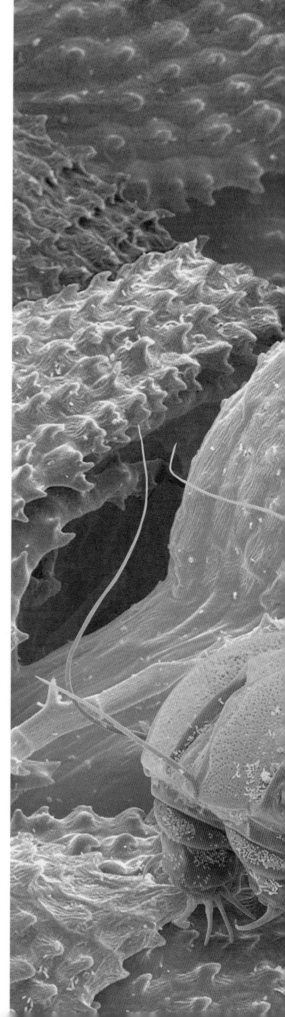

*Look into a microscope.*
*Tell me what you can see.*
*There's a tiny world in front of us,*
*full of tiny things to see.*

*Let's have a look!*

*My teacher said that creatures*
*smaller than a human hair*
*live in our world.*
*She said we'd find them everywhere!*

*Wow!*

*Some look like strange monsters,*
*with jaws and claws and horrible eyes.*
*But don't forget how small they are.*
*Don't forget their size.*

*CHORUS*

*Look a little bit closer!*

*There are tiny habitats*
*where predator and prey*
*have tiny little battles*
*every minute of the day.*

*Wow!*

*Mites live on our eyelashes.*
*That's just the way it goes.*
*What do they eat for breakfast?*
*Do you really want to know?*

*CHORUS*

*There's a tiny world in front of us,*
*full of tiny things to see.*

**5** **Tick T for *True* or F for *False*.**

1. Tiny creatures are everywhere. Ⓣ Ⓕ
2. Some creatures live on our jaws. Ⓣ Ⓕ
3. Small creatures never eat breakfast. Ⓣ Ⓕ

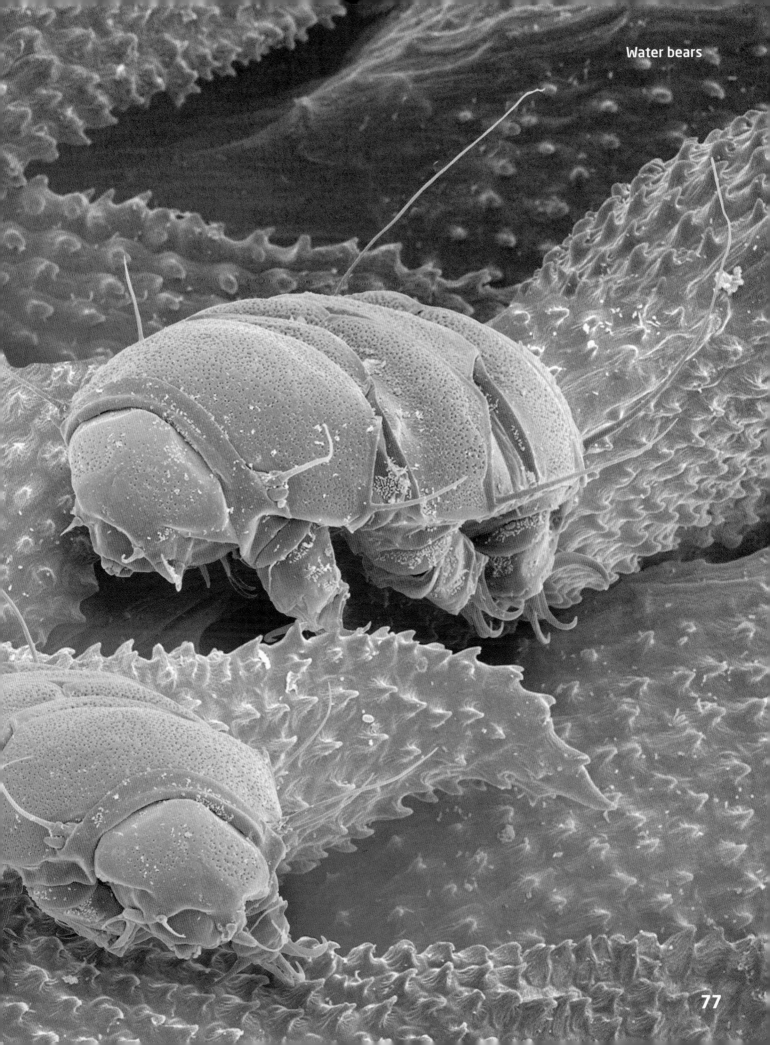

| | | |
|---|---|---|
| Dad: 'This sea horse **lives** near coral.' | → | My dad said that this sea horse **lived** near coral. |
| Mum: 'Eyelash mites **eat** dead skin cells.' | → | My mum said that eyelash mites **ate** dead skin cells. |
| Teacher: 'Hummingbirds **can't** smell.' | → | Our teacher said that hummingbirds **couldn't** smell. |
| Ben: 'You **are** wrong.' | → | Ben said that I **was** wrong. |

**6** **Read.** Report what your teacher told you. Write the reported sentences in your notebook.

1. 'An organism is a living thing. It can be a plant or an animal.'

2. 'Most organisms have more than one cell.'

3. 'The Denise sea horse isn't very common.'

4. 'The hummingbird lives near flowers, but it can't smell them.'

5. 'You can see an eyelash mite through a microscope.'

6. 'I don't like things that crawl on my head.'

**7** **What do you know?** Work with a friend. Say one fact about each creature. Use the prompts to help you. Your friend reports on what you said. Take turns.

female - male

eggs - beans

can move - wings

smaller - human's tooth

live - coral

male - babies

0.3 millimetres long

crawl - skin

eat - skin cell

**8** **Work in a group.** Write two true sentences and one false sentence. Read them to the group. Take turns.

Cats can't swim.

He said that cats couldn't swim, but they can!

**9** **Listen and repeat.** Look at the photos. Match. Complete
the sentences. **TR: A45**

**a. adult**

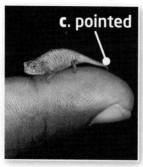
**c. pointed**

**b. tiny**          **d. furry**          **e. strange**

___a___ 1. That's so lovely. Look at how

the _____ elephant

is standing over the baby!

_____ 2. The _____ lizard is sitting

on a finger. It's so small!

_____ 3. The lizard has got a long _____ tail.

_____ 4. Can you see the _____ ladybird on the

blade of grass?

_____ 5. That little _____ monkey is beautiful.

_____ 6. Look at that _____ creature in the water.

Where is its head?

**f. spotted**

**10** **Work with a friend.** Talk and stick.
Take turns.

> This animal is soft and furry.

> It's a rabbit!

1   2   3   4   5

| Opinion | Size | Age | Shape | Colour | Pattern | Origin | Material | Thing |
|---------|------|-----|-------|--------|---------|--------|----------|-------|
| cute | | young | | | striped | | furry | creatures |
| | tiny | | pointed | grey | | | | ears |
| strange | | | | black | | Australian | hairy | spiders |
| common | | adult | | | spotted | | | bugs |

**11** **Read and write.** Describe the creatures.

1. These _____cute grey furry_____ animals are called marmosets.

   (furry / grey / cute)

2. The insect with the _____ antennae is a firefly.

   (pointed / long / black)

3. This _____ frog changes colour when it is scared.

   (adult / tiny / amazing)

4. The ladybird is a _____ bug.

   (spotted / red and black / common)

5. The Denise sea horse has got a _____ head.

   (pointed / strange / orange)

6. These eyelash mites are very _____ creatures.

   (transparent / tiny / ugly)

**12** **Play a game.** Cut out the game board and pictures on page 165. Choose eight of them for your game board. Listen and play bingo. TR: A47

There are about 1.5 million species on Earth, but how many do you see every day? You often see the big colourful animals, like birds, mammals and fish. But look more closely. Can you see the tiny creatures, too? Insects make up 80 per cent of the world's species. Look on the ground. Imagine you could look under the ground, too. Many organisms with one cell live there. Life is everywhere around us, in every cubic foot.

David Liittschwager is a photographer who wanted to find out how many creatures existed in one cubic foot. So he made a 12-inch cube with a green metal frame and put it in five habitats. He chose a tropical rainforest (Costa Rica), a coral reef (Pacific Ocean), Table Mountain (South Africa), a freshwater river (USA) and a city park (New York). Three weeks were spent at each site. He observed, counted and took photos of everything – down to one millimetre in size – that crawled or flew into the cube.

The results were amazing. Liittschwager found both common and rare creatures. He also discovered many new species, like a strange transparent octopus that is the size of a fingernail! In total, more than a thousand different organisms were photographed and analysed. Liittschwager said the One Cubic Foot experience was like 'finding treasure'. Although the coral reef had the widest range of biodiversity, all the other habitats were full of life. Even the city park!

**transparent octopus**

1 foot (ft.) =
12 inches (in.)
0.3048 metres (m.)
30.48 centimetres (cm.)

**14** **Read and write.** Underline the best title for the text. Write it in the title box.

A Biography of David Liittschwager

Life Is Everywhere

How to Do a 'One Cubic Foot' Project

**15** **Read.** Match each word or phrase with its correct meaning.

1. one cubic foot        a. to watch

2. rare        b. a place where living and non-living things exist together

3. biodiversity        c. 12 inches x 12 inches x 12 inches

4. an ecosystem        d. the variety of life on Earth

5. to observe        e. not common

**16** **Work with a friend.** Read the text again. Ask and answer questions. Use the answers in the cube.

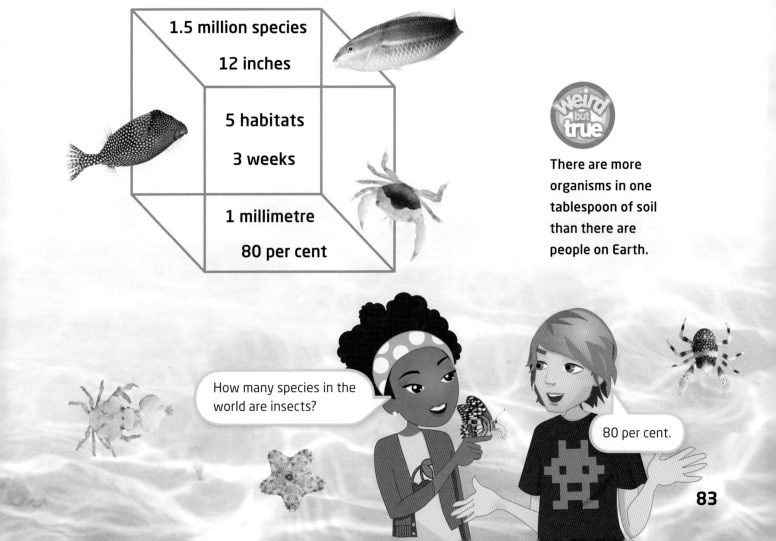

1.5 million species

12 inches

5 habitats

3 weeks

1 millimetre

80 per cent

**Weird but true**

There are more organisms in one tablespoon of soil than there are people on Earth.

How many species in the world are insects?

80 per cent.

## Science Reports

When you write a science report, include statistics and details. For example, if you are writing about an animal, include its scientific name, information about its habitat, food and other characteristics, as well as expert opinions. You can also use words that describe size, shape, colour, pattern and origin.

**17** **Read.** Read the report. Number the order in which you find the information on the list below (1-6).

___ food

___ an interesting fact

___ conclusion

_1_ scientific name

___ habitat

___ physical characteristics

## An interesting sea creature

Denise's pygmy sea horse (scientific name: Hippocampus denise) is a species of fish that is found in Asia. The natural habitat of H. denise is coral reefs, where it uses camouflage to hide. H. denise eats soft coral and is found at a depth of 13–90 metres.

H. denise is light orange in colour, with a strange head that resembles a horse and a long, thin, pointed tail. It grows to a total length of 16 millimetres (about 0.6 inches). According to the Australian biologist Rudie Kuiter, it is so small that it can escape from predators.

An interesting characteristic of the Denise sea horse is that males have the babies, not females. Males can carry 10–1,000 babies during their lives. Because the Denise sea horse uses camouflage to hide and lives so deep in the corals, scientists hope it is safe from problems other sea horses face.

**18** **Write.** Write an animal report. Include statistics, facts and an expert opinion. Remember to use descriptive words.

**19** **Work in a small group.** Share your writing.

# Mission

## Be curious.

- Scientists have recently discovered this new species, the mouse lemur. Work in a small group. Make a list of things you would like to know about this animal. Discuss.

- How could you find the answers to your questions? Discuss and write your best ideas in the box.

*'The more questions I asked, the more it became clear to me that much about our natural world still remained a mystery.'*

**Mireya Mayor**
**Primatologist/Conservationist**
Emerging Explorer

We could do some research on the Internet.

_____

_____

_____

_____

- Work with another group. Share your ideas. Are they the same or different? Which ideas does everyone like best?

## 20 Research two related animals.

1. Choose two related animals: one large and one small. For example, you might choose a tiger and a cat.

2. Research the two animals.

3. Make a poster about the two animals.

   a. Write a short summary about the animals. What have they got in common? How are they different?

   b. Add photos and pictures showing where the animals live.

The huge h
The Patu Di
of a pin! Th
in the swan
the size of
eats the n

These two spiders are very different!

...Goliath Birdeater Spider is one of biggest spiders in the world.
...pider is one of the smallest spiders. It is smaller than the head
...k brown Goliath Birdeater Spider is a kind of tarantula and is found
... South America. It grows to a length of about 30.5 cm. [about 12 inches],
...all pizza. It doesn't eat birds or humans, but sometimes the female

abdomen

eyes

Goliath Birdeater Spider

The Patu Digua Spider is this small!

Patu Digua Spider

**Now I can ...**

○ identify small creatures and their characteristics.

○ describe creatures.

○ report what other people say.

○ write a science report.

# Good Choice

In this unit, I will ...
- talk about products and their characteristics.
- talk about preferences.
- report commands and questions.
- write a product review.

**Answer the question.**

What is the most important thing to consider when you buy a product?

Order them 1–4. (1 = most important)

____ a good price      ____ useful
____ good quality      ____ good design

**1** **Listen and read.** TR: B2

**2** **Listen and repeat.** TR: B3

Have you ever bought a **product** that **broke** the next day? It's not fair, especially if it **cost** a lot of money! It's also bad for the **manufacturer**. Unhappy **customers** tell many people if a product isn't good **quality**!

Most manufacturers **test** their products carefully before selling them. Cars must pass **safety** tests. To test a car, they put **dummies**, which look like humans, inside the car. Then, they make the car crash. **Crash tests** show manufacturers what happens on **impact**.

Toys are tested, too. The 'torque test' twists toys until they break. The 'drop test' **drops** toys on the floor. **Waterproof** toys are **dipped** in water. Machines **tear** balloons. If something doesn't work, manufacturers have to **fix** the problem.

**3** **Work with a friend.** What did you learn? Ask and answer.

What happens when customers are unhappy with a product?

They tell lots of people.

## 4 Listen, read and sing. TR: B4

# Safe Buys

*Lots of the things we buy*
*are tested for safety.*
*That's good! Products should be safe.*
*They should be safe for you and me.*

*When you're a customer,*
*the products you buy shouldn't break.*
*A manufacturer*
*should try not to make mistakes.*

*Is this watch waterproof?*
*It goes tick tock.*
*Let's dip the watch in water!*
*It's just a test to make sure everything is safe.*

*CHORUS*

*Quality is important.*
*Products should be safe.*
*A factory that makes things*
*should test everything, just in case.*

*A dummy sits in a car.*
*The car speeds up!*
*Crash! Don't worry!*
*It's just a test to make sure everything is safe.*

*CHORUS*

*Safe for you and me!*

## 5 Complete the sentences. Answer.

1a. The two products tested in the song are a

watch and _____.

1b. We test products so that they are

_____ for people.

2. Have you ever bought anything that broke?
What happened?

92

'**Put** your pen in your rucksack.'
'**Don't break** my toys.'

Mum told me **to put** my pen in my rucksack.
My brother told me **not to break** his toys.

**6** **Read.** Your friends lent you a toy. Write their instructions about the toy. Circle the toy.

1. 'Look after it.'        _They told me to look after it._

2. 'Don't drop it.'        _____

3. 'Don't tear its clothes.'   _____

4. 'Don't twist its arms.'     _____

5. 'Enjoy it.'             _____

**7** **What about you?** Imagine your friends want to use some of your things. Tell them what to do and what not to do.

**Your rucksack**

1. _____
2. _____
3. _____

**Your new pen**

1. _____
2. _____
3. _____

**Your bicycle**

1. _____
2. _____
3. _____

**8** **Work in a group.** Compare your ideas. Are they the same or different?

I told Matt not to tear my rucksack.

I did, too. And I told him not to give it to anyone.

**9** **Listen and repeat.** Read and complete the paragraph. TR: B6

reception

Wi-Fi

an app

a text message

a key

wear and tear

This is a great mobile phone for young people who only need to make phone calls
and send _____. It does not have _____,
so you can't send emails. The phone has a cool design and comes in many colours.
Also, it will survive lots of _____. Tests show that it does
not break if you drop it. The screen is large and the _____
are easy to press. The _____ is good in most places.
Young people might prefer a mobile phone that comes with games and other
_____, but this is a great simple phone.

**10** **Work with a friend.**
Listen and stick.
Compare your answers. TR: B7

How do manufacturers test the keys?

They press them thousands of times for five days.

Yes, I've got the same answer.

## GRAMMAR TR: B8

| | |
|---|---|
| Lisa: '**What** do I need to do next?' | Lisa asked me **what** she **needed** to do next. |
| Ken: '**Can** you help me?' | Ken asked me **if** I **could** help him. |

**11** **Read.** Look at the pictures. Follow the model. Write in your notebook.

1. _The woman asked him if she could help him._

**12** **Play a memory game.** Cut out the cards on page 167. Play in a small group.

97

# Be an Ad Detective!

Every day we see adverts – on TV, in magazines, on websites, in the street and on our computer screens. We hear them, too. But often we don't notice them. A famous film producer once showed over 100 products in his film, but most people didn't notice them!

Are you an ad detective? Can you understand the messages advertisers send you? To be an ad detective, it is useful to know how ads work. Let's look at some typical advertising techniques.

1.  **Group pressure:** An ad shows lots of young people, each with their own mobile phone. Message: Everyone has a mobile phone. You need one, too!

2.  **Association:** Everyone looks happy and healthy in the ad. They're cool and beautiful, too. Message: If you buy the product, you will be happy and cool like these people.

3.  **Testimonials:** A famous athlete says he wears a certain brand of trainers. Message: You'll be good at sports, too, if you buy these trainers. Or, because a famous athlete wears these trainers, they're a product you can trust.

4.  **Repetition:** These ads mention the product many times and say wonderful things about it. Message: You need to remember the product.

5.  **Time pressure:** These ads use expressions like 'Buy now! Half price this week.' Message: You should buy the product quickly before you miss a great opportunity.

Adverts are interesting, but you can make better decisions about what to buy when you know these techniques! Try these tips: read product reviews, compare products, test products in the store and, if you are not sure, wait 24 hours before buying. You may decide that you don't really need or want the product!

headline — **BOUNDLESS BMX...**

visual —

Professional BMX biker Mario 'Hot-Rod' Rodriguez says, 'When I want to ride extreme, I ride a *Boundless BMX*. I flip, drop and always land on top, with low impact. *Boundless BMX*–just ride it.'

copy —

**Just ride it!**

**BOUNDLESS BMX**

tagline          logo

**14** **Read.** Re-read the text. Find the technique used in each ad below. Write the number.

a. __3__ A popular hip-hop singer is advertising some clothes.

b. _____ Summer holidays end next week. Rucksacks are half price this week.

c. _____ You hear the name of the product seven times in a 30-second ad.

d. _____ Some friends are playing outdoors. They're all wearing the same trainers.

e. _____ Young people are cycling outdoors. They're laughing. The sun is shining.

**15** **Read the text again.** Find other word forms.

1. advertisement   ⟶   _____ _ad_ _____

2. decide   ⟶   _____

3. producer   ⟶   _____

4. repeat   ⟶   _____

**16** **Work with a friend.** Look at the tips in the last paragraph. Discuss. Which is:

1. the most useful tip?
2. a tip you already use?
3. a tip you would never use?
4. a tip you would like to try?

**Weird but true**

The time shown on most watches in ads is 10.10. This is because the hands of the watch in this position look like a smiling face.

I think the most useful tip is to wait 24 hours.

Me, too. I always buy things too quickly!

99

## Product Reviews

In a product review, you help the customer decide what to buy. It is not an advert, so you can describe both the positive and negative aspects of the product. To emphasise the good points, use expressions like *above all, particularly, of course, in fact, really, the truth is* and *in addition*.

**17** **Read.** Read the review. Underline the expressions that the writer uses to emphasise the positive features of the rucksack.

### Carry your books in style

This is a good quality rucksack for school children aged 11 to 13 who need to carry a lot of books. It is made of strong material that will survive a lot of wear and tear. In fact, we tested it and it doesn't tear easily. In addition, the material is waterproof, so children's books won't get wet in the rain.

We particularly like this rucksack because it doesn't weigh a lot. Of course, leather rucksacks may look cooler, but they are heavier. Carrying a heavy rucksack is bad for your back, so the truth is, we prefer this one.

Above all, we like that the rucksack comes in many colours and designs. The only problem? The straps are a little short. So we suggest that you try it on in the shop before you decide. We give this rucksack four stars.****

**18** **Write.** Review a product. Write about why you like it and make a recommendation. Use expressions of emphasis for the good points.

**19** **Share your work with a small group.** Listen and make notes.

| Name | Product | Good points | Bad points | Number of stars |
|------|---------|-------------|------------|-----------------|
|      |         |             |            |                 |
|      |         |             |            |                 |

# NATIONAL GEOGRAPHIC
# Mission

## Be aware of why you are making decisions.

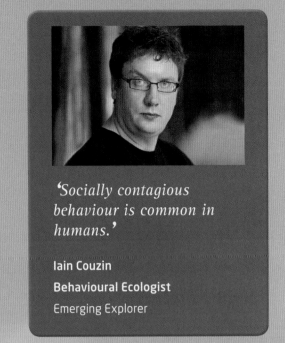

'*Socially contagious behaviour is common in humans.*'

Iain Couzin
Behavioural Ecologist
Emerging Explorer

Work in a small group. Think of the things you own. Why did you or your parent buy them? How did you feel when you bought them? How did you feel a month later?

Have you ever bought something just because your friends have it? Why? Write some examples.

I bought a computer game because my
friend said it was good. I didn't enjoy it!

• Work with another group. Share your examples. Are they the same or different? Which product was a good idea to buy? Which one was a bad idea? Discuss why.

**20** **Make a collage of ads.**

1. Choose a product. Cut out advertisements that sell your product.

2. Analyse the ads.

   a. Who is responsible for the ad? What are they advertising?

   b. Who is the advertiser selling the product to?

   c. What techniques does the ad use?

   d. What does the ad say or suggest about the product?

3. Make a collage using the ads.

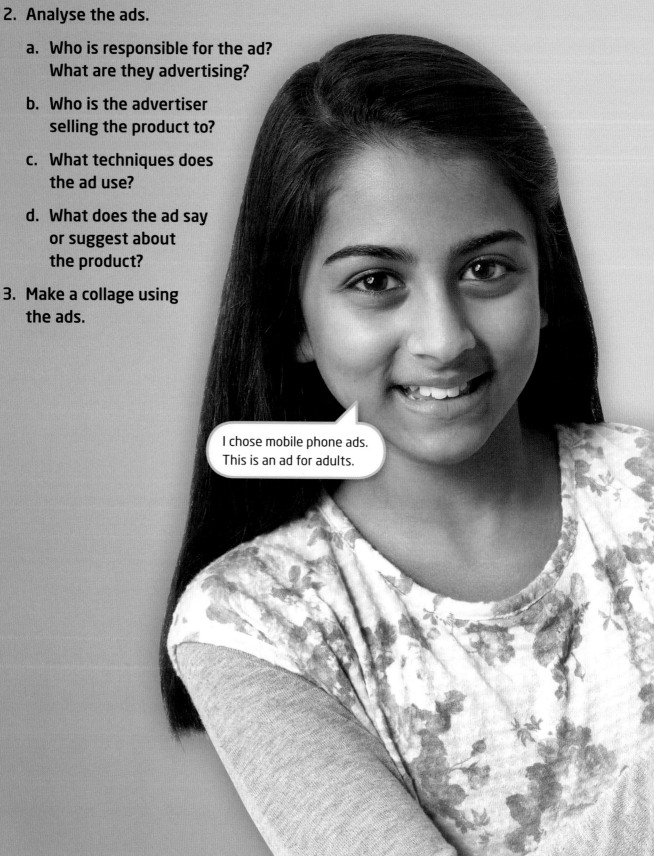

I chose mobile phone ads. This is an ad for adults.

**FOR US**
great for texting

**Got2Go**

"Hey! How R U? ☺"

Plus, our cool phones come in pretty pink, bright blue and green and even sunny yellow!

cool colours

Sakura uses her new **Got2Go** mobile phone to text all her friends, and so can you!

Got2Go

**FOR MUM AND DAD**

lots of apps

7:27 PM

**GET THE MESSAGE**

Get the Message mobile phones are on sale today! We test all our products and are proud to offer waterproof keys, great reception and free apps! Buy a new mobile phone today — get the message?

**FOR GRANDMA AND GRANDDAD**

Are you tired of your mobile phone's small screen and tiny text messages? At **Clear Keys**, our phones are made with larger keys for typing and wider, easy-to-see screens!

**Clear Keys**

very big keys

## Now I can ...

- ◯ talk about products and their characteristics.
- ◯ talk about preferences.
- ◯ report commands and questions.
- ◯ write a product review.

**1** **Listen.** What kind of mobile phone has Jenny bought?
Tick the features. TR: B10

○ email     ○ text messages     ○ nice colour     ○ strong keys

○ big screen     ○ Wi-Fi     ○ games / apps

**2** **Listen.** Number the sentences. TR: B11

____ I told them that it cost me money.

____ I'll ask my son not to take it for a swim next time!

____ The shop assistant said that they tested everything.

__1__ Did you ask the shop assistant if it was waterproof?

____ They told me to buy another one!

____ Did you ask them if they could fix it?

**3** **Work with a friend.** You want to return or exchange the broken phone.
Act out a conversation.

> Hello. Can I help you?

> Yes, please. Yesterday I bought a mobile phone in this shop and ...

**4** **Work in groups of three.** Take turns. Ask and answer questions. Make notes.

1. Have you ever visited a waterfall or a lake? Where?
2. Which water creatures do you find interesting? Why?
3. How do you try to save water at home?
4. If you saw someone wasting water right now, what would you tell them?
5. Whenever you see a leaking tap, what do you do?
6. Have you been swimming recently? Did you swim in salt water or in fresh water?

**5** **Work with another group.** Compare your information. How are you similar and different?

So how are we different?

Well, I've been to the Angel Falls!

And we haven't. But we've been to lots of lakes!

**6** **Read.** Match the questions and answers. Then put the words in brackets in order.

QUESTIONS

1. Tiny bugs have been crawling on old books in our study. My son said they were booklice. Are there really booklice? What are they?

2. My daughter said that head lice only lived in dirty hair. Is this true?

ANSWERS

A: ____ No. They like all kinds, clean and dirty! However, these (grey / tiny / common) _____ insects prefer children between the age of four and eleven! They've got long legs that help them crawl on human heads.

B: ____ He's right. These (brown / strange / light) _____ organisms usually live outdoors, but some other habitats include libraries, cupboards and other warm indoor places. Adults reach lengths of 1-2 millimetres.

**7** **Write.** Imagine you are a very small insect. Write a fun question about humans. Then write a short description of a human!

# Let's Talk

## I mean ...

I will ...
- ask a friend for help.
- give myself time to think.
- correct myself.
- show doubt.

**1** **Listen and read.** TR: B12

Thomas: **Can you help me with** my homework?
**I'm confused.**

Paul: **Sure**, Thomas. **What's the problem**?

Thomas: What's the difference between a
tornado and a thunderstorm? **I don't get it**.

Paul: **Well**, tornadoes bring heavy rain. **I mean**, they
bring a lot of *wind*, not rain.

John: Yes. And the wind moves very quickly in a circle.

Paul: But a thunderstorm is different. There's lots of rain.

Thomas: **Are you sure**? **I always thought that** thunderstorms had lots of wind, too.

| | | | |
|---|---|---|---|
| Can you help me with _____ ?<br>**I'm confused.**<br>**I don't get it.** | **Sure. What's the problem**?<br>Of course! Tell me. | **Well**, ...<br>**I mean**, ...<br>Let me think.<br>Hang on.<br>Um ... | **Are you sure**?<br>Is that right?<br>I don't think so.<hr>**I always thought that** ...<br>I read that ...<br>I heard that ...<br>_____ told me that ... |

**2** **Work in groups of three.** Use the table. Discuss English
words that you often find confusing. For example:

*history* and *story*     *alone* and *lonely*     *fun* and *funny*

106

# Actually, it's true.

I will ...
- express surprise and disbelief.
- contest a fact.
- quote a source.
- agree to disagree / concede.

**3** **Listen and read.** TR: D13

Julia: Why don't we write about ants? There are more than 16,000 species of ants on the planet. And they're cool!

Leyla: No way! **Where did you get that idea**?

Julia: **Actually**, **it's true**. And **according to the scientist Edward O. Wilson**, there might be even more species than that.

Leyla: **OK**, let's write about ants **then**!

| **Where did you get that idea**? I can't believe that! Sorry, but I can't see how that's possible. | **Actually, it's true**. You know, there are many sources. In fact, that's right. | **According to** _____ , Research shows that ... A study by _____ shows that ... | **OK**. **OK**, _____ **then**! Alright. Let's ... That's interesting. I've never thought about that before. |
| --- | --- | --- | --- |

**4** **Listen.** You will hear two discussions. Circle the answer. TR: B14

1. Who or what do the students quote?
   a. a website   b. a study   c. an explorer   d. their teacher

2. Who or what do the students quote?
   a. a website   b. a study   c. an explorer   d. their teacher

**5** **Work with a friend.** Choose a situation and discuss.

1. I heard on TV that chocolate is good for you. Let's write about that.

2. Why don't we do a report on 'BASE jumping'? You know, about 200 people have died doing this sport. I read it in a magazine.

3. Let's do a project on ancient Egypt. There are lots of articles on the National Geographic website about it.

# Unit 7

# Wonders of the Natural World

In this unit, I will ...
- describe natural places.
- talk about safety rules.
- talk about feelings.
- write a chronological narrative.

**Tick T for *True* or F for *False*.**

1. There are three explorers in the cave.   (T) (F)

2. The water is flowing very fast.   (T) (F)

3. Their work is probably dangerous.   (T) (F)

Ora Cave, New Britain Island,
Papua New Guinea

**1** **Listen and read.** TR: B15

**2** **Listen and repeat.** TR: B16

Explorers have dangerous jobs. They hike through jungles, **ascend** and **descend** steep mountains, or swim with sharks. They take big **risks** to learn more about our world.

Whenever Kenny Broad descends into a deep saltwater cave, he takes risks. Poisonous **underwater** gases fill the air. Broad needs **safety equipment**. He wears a helmet for protection and uses a **headlamp** to **shine** on the cave. The **rope** helps him find his way.

Dan's Cave, Abaco Island,
Bahama Islands

Mireya Mayor is an outdoor scientist who observes wildlife. To find gorillas, she **crosses streams**, climbs mountains and crawls along **tunnels**. Her work is sometimes very dangerous. Once she was even **chased** by a gorilla! Mayor believes anyone with **curiosity** can be an explorer.

Matthew Berger, son of famous explorer Lee Berger, made an amazing discovery in South Africa **by accident**. Nine-year-old Matthew was running after his dog when he **tripped over** and **located** the two-million-year-old fossil of a boy.

**3** **Work with a friend.** What did you learn? Ask and answer.

What does Kenny Broad explore?

Underwater caves.

## 4 Listen, read and sing. TR: B17

# Let's Explore

*Let's go exploring!*

**Let's explore! Let's go inside a cave.**
**Let's explore! Make sure that you're safe.**
**Let's explore! There's so much to see.**
**Don't forget your safety equipment and curiosity!**

*We're inside a cave.*
*We're ready to climb down.*
*What should we use to keep us safe?*
*A rope can be used to help us descend.*
*A headlamp can be worn to help us light our way.*

**CHORUS**

*We're deep underwater*
*and we'd like to ascend.*
*What should we use to help us stay safe?*
*A rope can be used to help us ascend.*
*Let's follow it to find our way back to where we*
*began.*

*When we're underwater in the jungle or in a cave,*
*safety equipment must be used to help us stay safe.*

**CHORUS**

*Let's explore!*

## 5 Answer the questions.

1. What two things should we take with us when we explore?
   a. safety equipment   b. _____

2. Tick the safety equipment that is not mentioned in the song.
   a. __ a headlamp   b. __ a rope   c. __ a helmet

3. Would you like to explore a cave? Why or why not? What place would you most like to explore?

_____

Cave of Swallows, Mexico

Headlamps **must be worn** in dark caves.
Dangerous places **mustn't be entered** alone.

New species **have to be studied** in a science lab.
They **can't be analysed** underwater.

**6** **Read and write.** Complete the paragraph.

The Nyiragongo volcano is beautiful but dangerous. If it erupts, it could

kill the people who live below it. The people (1) ___must be helped___ (must /

help). When a volcano starts to erupt, it (2) _____

(can't / stop). To save lives, volcanic activity (3) _____

(have to / study). Rocks (4) _____ (have to / collect)

from inside the volcano. That's a job for volcanologist, Ken Sims. Before

Sims and his team descend, they need safety equipment. The safety

equipment (5) _____ (have to / check). Rubber shoes

(6) _____ (shouldn't / use) because they melt in the heat!

Special suits and gas masks (7) _____ (have to / wear) to

protect the scientists against heat and poisonous gases. As Sims descends by

rope, the sound of gases (8) _____ (can / hear) below. It's

scary. But he collects the rocks and ascends safely. Now he

and other scientists can learn more about the volcano.

**7** **What do you think?** Write safety rules for tourists who visit these places. Use these words.

| volcano<br>jungle<br>mountain<br>underwater cave | environment<br>risks<br>animals<br>headlamp<br>photos<br>water | suit<br>water<br>food<br>boots<br>helmet<br>rope | wear<br>carry<br>protect<br>use<br>take<br>drink |
|---|---|---|---|

1. In the jungle, boots must be worn. _____

2. _____

3. _____

4. _____

5. _____

6. _____

**8** **Work in a group.** Compare your rules.

In an underwater cave, a headlamp must be worn.

A rope can be used to help you descend.

**9** **Listen and repeat.** Look at the pictures. Complete the paragraph. TR: B19

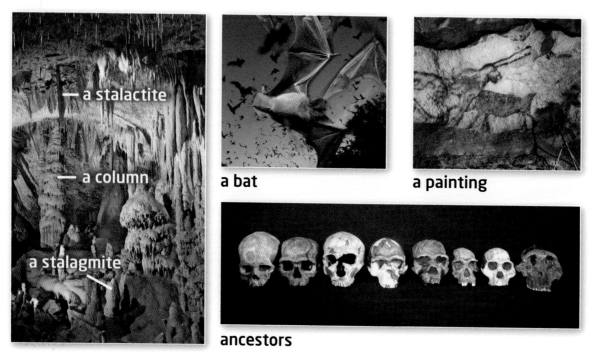

a stalactite
a column
a stalagmite

a bat

a painting

ancestors

Caves are full of life, such as bears, snakes and (1) _____. Caves
used to be full of human life, too. We know that our (2) _____
lived in caves thousands of years ago because they made (3) _____
on the cave walls. In caves, water drips through the rocks to form stalactites and
(4) _____. They grow slowly. When a stalactite and stalagmite
meet, they form a (5) _____. This can take thousands of years!
Here is an easy way to remember the difference. Stalagmites rise from the <u>g</u>round.
(6) _____ hang from the <u>c</u>eiling!

**10** **Listen and stick.** Work with a friend. TR: B20

1     2     3     4     5

Caves **make me** scared.
Heights **made her** nervous.

Exploring **makes Mireya** happy.
Matthew Berger **made his dad** proud.

**11** **Read.** Write sentences. Write about you, your family and your friends.

| proud   scared   happy   sick   nervous   angry   tired   hungry |

1. *Thinking about chocolate makes me hungry!*

2. _____

3. _____

4. _____

5. _____

6. _____

**12** **Play a game.** Make the cubes on page 169. Play with a friend. Take turns. Make sentences.

*Happy, bats, me.* Bats make me happy!

That's really funny! My turn.

# Discoveries in the Dark

Explorer David Gill and his team are studying the beautiful island of New Britain, in Papua New Guinea. Some of the biggest river caves on Earth can be found here. During their two-month expedition, the team explores 13 kilometres (eight miles) of river caves, discovering waterfalls, lakes and much more!

The team makes a base camp at the top of the 'doline' (a large bowl carved by rainwater). They sleep here, surrounded by rainforest and the sounds of frogs and insects. To reach Ora Cave, the explorers must descend the doline. Before entering the caves, they check their safety equipment. They need headlamps to explore the dark world of river caves. And they can't cross rivers without ropes.

Ora's upstream hike is difficult and the river flows dangerously fast. Eventually it leads to a large cave, as big as a theatre! The explorers shine their headlamps on the ceiling, which is more than 30 metres (100 feet) high. A beautiful blue lake lies below. Unfortunately, the explorers can't hike to Phantom Pot from Ora Cave because there is a rocky 'sump' (an area where water drains back into the earth). So they have to descend another day to Phantom Pot Cave. This time, the explorers crawl for two hours through a tiny rocky tunnel. When they reach Lake Myo and the Myo Falls, they are tired and wet, but the view is truly incredible!

David Gill hopes that one day the Papua New Guinea government will create a conservation area to protect this wonderful place.

**Weird but true**

The Cave of Crystals in Mexico contains the world's largest natural crystals – one is as big as a school bus!

## 14 Read and write.

1. How long do the explorers spend on New Britain Island? _____

2. What safety equipment do they use? _____

3. Why can't they hike directly from Ora Cave to Phantom Pot Cave?

_____

4. How can the government protect this island in the future?

_____

## 15 Read the text again. Look at the cave diagram. Number the places below. Write 1-6.

_____ base camp          _____ doline          ___l___ underground river

_____ Lake Myo           _____ sump            _____ rainforest

## 16 Work with a friend. Discuss some risks that the explorers could face on different parts of their journey. Compare your ideas with another pairs' ideas.

The explorers could fall in the river.

They might also lose their equipment in the river!

## Chronological Narratives

When you write a chronological narrative, you describe when each event happened. To make the story more interesting, you can set the scene and create suspense. To express the sequence of events, you can use time expressions such as *ago*, *afterwards*, *immediately*, *suddenly* or *then*.

**17** **Read.** Which time expression is not used in the narrative? How does the writer create suspense?

### Search for a gorilla

A few years ago, the explorer Mireya Mayor visited a jungle in Africa because she wanted to learn more about female gorillas. She joined some other scientists who were studying a male called 'Kingo'. Together they followed the gorillas everywhere. It was incredibly hot and the trail was difficult. First, there were bees in her face. Then, she had to hike through mud for hours. At one point, when she was hiking through mud, she fell. She grabbed a tree, but she didn't know that there were ants in the tree. Hundreds of ants fell on her head and they were crawling through her hair! They crawled under her clothes and bit her many times. It was horrible. But something amazing happened. Suddenly, she heard a female gorilla scream. She felt so excited. This was the female she wanted to find! She immediately forgot about bees, mud and ants and ran to find the gorilla. It was one of the most exciting moments of her life!

**18** **Write.** Imagine you are an explorer. Write about an adventure you had in a cave, a volcano or the jungle. Remember to create suspense and describe the sequence of events.

**19** **Work in a small group.** Share your writing.

# NATIONAL GEOGRAPHIC
# Mission

## Connect your school studies to the world.

- Work in a small group. Discuss what you have learnt in Science and Geography recently.

- How are these topics useful in the real world? Write some ideas in the box.

*'I am inspired by nature and I try to take what I learn about nature and apply those lessons to design things people can use and to help us understand more about the world we live in.'*

**Kakani Katija, Bioengineer**
Emerging Explorer

We learnt about the Amazon rainforest.

It's important because it helps maintain our

climate.

- Work with another group. Share your ideas. Are they the same or different? Which ideas does everyone like best?

Mosaic jellyfish,
New South Wales, Australia

## 20 Make a diorama.

1. Work in a group of three.

2. Research some caves in the world.
   Choose one that interests you.

3. Learn how to make a cave diorama.

4. Find the materials you need.

5. Make the cave.

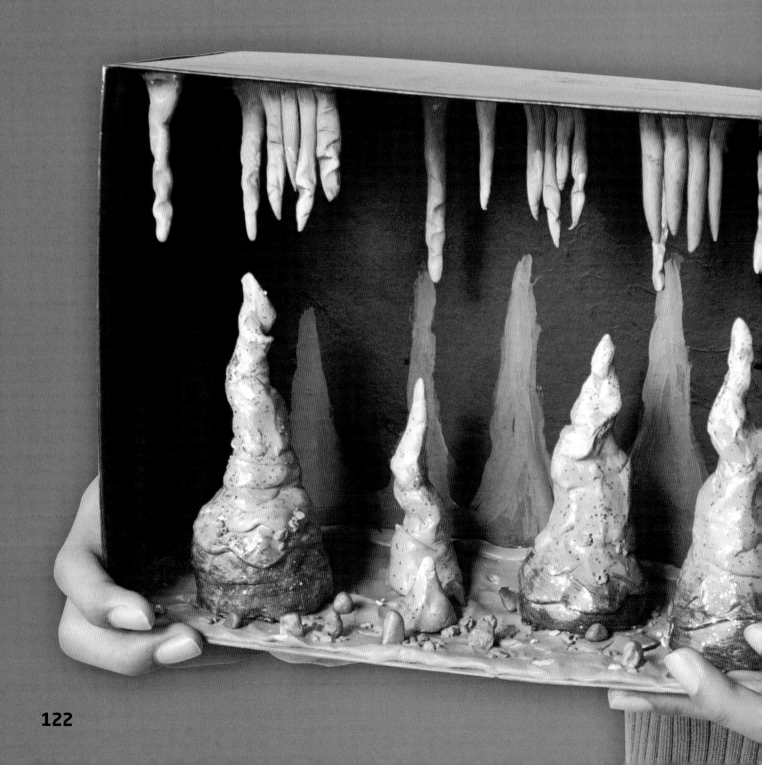

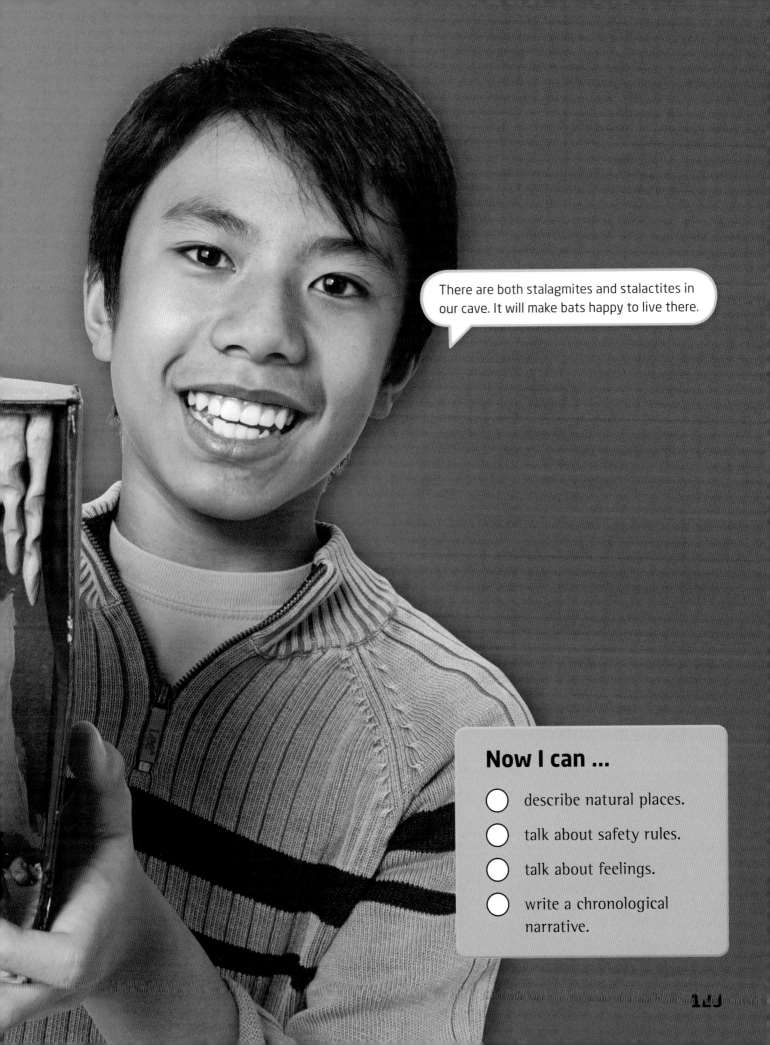

There are both stalagmites and stalactites in our cave. It will make bats happy to live there.

## Now I can ...

- ◯ describe natural places.
- ◯ talk about safety rules.
- ◯ talk about feelings.
- ◯ write a chronological narrative.

# Robots Rule

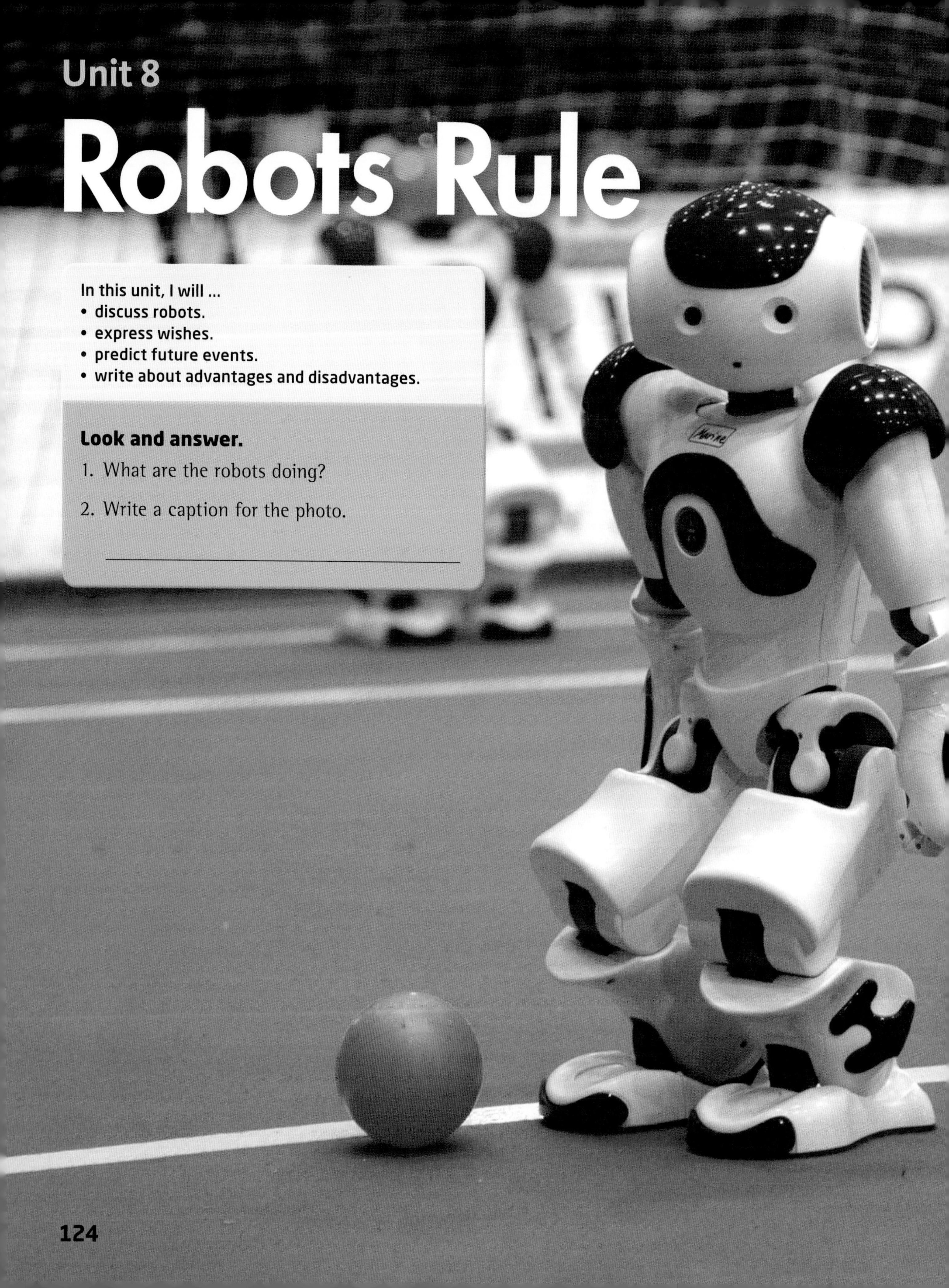

In this unit, I will ...
• discuss robots.
• express wishes.
• predict future events.
• write about advantages and disadvantages.

**Look and answer.**

1. What are the robots doing?

2. Write a caption for the photo.

_____

Robots playing football during RoboCup

## 1 **Listen and read.** TR: B23

## 2 **Listen and repeat.** TR: B24

Robots (or 'bots') are not just in **science fiction** films. In real life, they work in many environments – in space, on land and underwater. They do amazing jobs!

SPACE    Robots can explore space easily because they are **mobile** and extremely **precise**. Also, they never need food or sleep. 'Bots' have successfully visited Mars, Venus and Jupiter, where they were **controlled** by humans on Earth using **remote controls**.

**Mars Rover**

EARTH On Earth, robots are often used to perform useful **tasks** like cleaning and shopping. Robovie II is a Japanese shopping robot that helps people at the supermarket. Robots perform **social** tasks, too. For example, AIBO the dog is a wonderful **companion** for people. TOPIO, an android robot with human **features**, can even play table tennis.

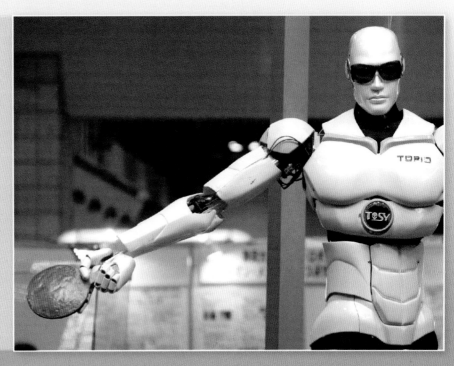

UNDERWATER Bots do tasks that are too **dangerous** or **complex** for humans. They can **respond to commands** underwater, like collecting **information** about sea life. Scientists hope to be able to **program** them to clean oil spills, too. Can robots help us save our seas?

**3** **Work with a friend.** What did you learn? Ask and answer.

Have robots been to Jupiter?

Yes, they have. They've been to Mars and Venus, too.

# I Am a Robot

*If I were a robot, what would my life be like?*
*I wish I were a robot! What would that life be like?*

*Now, I am a robot. I follow all commands.*
*But I wish I had more features.*
*I wish I had better hands.*

*Now, I am a robot. I do what I am told.*
*But I wish I had a birthday.*
*Then again, I will never get old.*

**I am a robot. I can do so many things.**
**Have you ever met a robot that can sing?**

*Now, I am a robot. I'm helpful and I'm clever.*
*But I wish that I could fix myself. I sometimes fall apart.*

*Now, I am a robot, made of wires and steel.*
*I'll always say the same thing if you ask me how I feel.*

***CHORUS***

*Now, I am a robot and I must say goodbye.*
*But even when I'm sad, I am programmed not to cry.*

***CHORUS***

*Have you ever met a robot that can sing?*

**5** **Answer the questions.**

1. Circle things that this robot would like to be able to do.
   a. follow commands
   b. have a birthday
   c. cry

2. Discuss. In what ways are robots similar to humans? In what ways are they different?

3. Discuss. Would you like to be a robot? Why or why not?

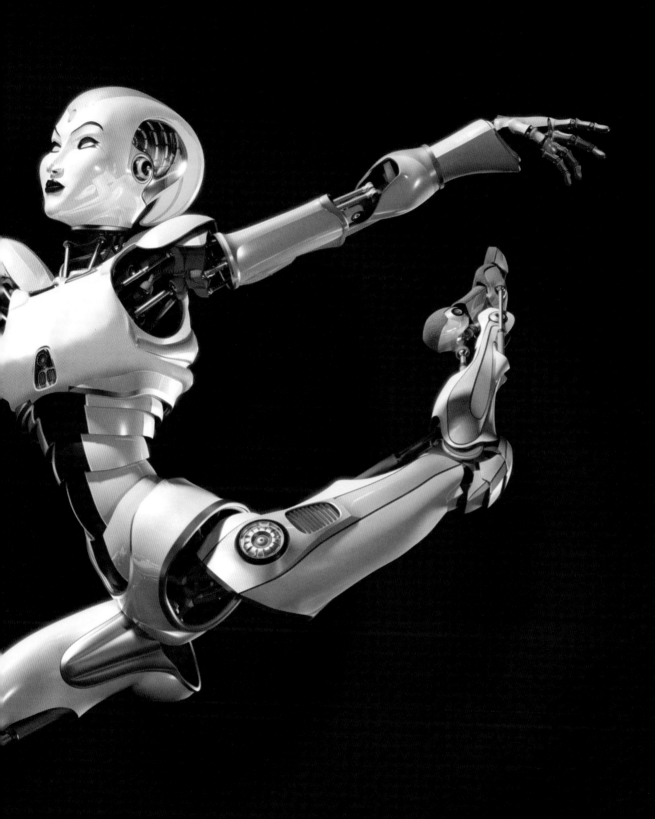

I wish my teacher **were** a robot. (But my teacher is not a robot!)
I wish I **could** program a robot. (But I can't.)
Dad wishes he **had** a robot that played table tennis! (But he hasn't got one.)
Mum wishes the vacuuming robot **didn't cost** so much. (But it costs a lot.)

**6** **Read and write.** Complete the sentences.

1. I _____wish_____ a personal robot _____could help_____ (can / help) me speak English.

2. My family _____ there _____ (be) a robot to cook for us.

3. I _____ I _____ (not / have) to do everything myself. I'd like a personal robot!

4. My sister _____ she _____ (have) a robot to make snacks for her.

5. I _____ robots _____ (not / be) so expensive.

6. My cousins _____ they _____ (have) robots to make their beds!

7. I _____ I _____ (can) play table tennis like TOPIO.

8. Our cat _____ my mum _____ (not / use) a vacuuming robot. He gets scared!

**7** **What about you?** What do you wish a robot could do for you? For other people? For plants and animals?

For me:   _I wish a robot could explain my homework to me._

_____

_____

_____

For other people:   _I wish my grandmother had a robot shopper._

_____

_____

_____

For plants and animals:   _I wish a robot could water the plants when we are on_

_holiday._

_____

_____

**8** **Work with a friend.** Compare your wishes.

I wish a robot carried my books to school!

I wish a robot carried me to school!

**9** **Listen and repeat.** Then listen and underline the missing words. TR: B27

# NEW! 'Robo-Friend'

## The new 'Robo-Friend' has many exciting features:

She's got **voice recognition.** She can understand you when you speak!

She's got **facial recognition,** too. When she sees your face, she knows who you are.

Hundreds of **lasers** tell 'Robo-Friend' what is in front of her, so she doesn't trip over.

She's got a **mechanical** arm. She can lift things for you.

She's got thousands of **sensors.** She can feel, smell and touch things.

1. sensors / voice recognition
2. mechanical / voice recognition
3. facial recognition / lasers
4. mechanical / lasers

**10** **Listen and stick.** Work with a friend. Discuss. TR: B28

Tell me about ASIMO. What can it do?

It's got facial recognition. It can recognise the faces of ten people.

Robots **will be programmed** to do many of our dangerous jobs one day.
Most people **won't be required** to work more than a few hours a week.

**11** **Read and answer.** Complete the sentences about robots in the classroom. Tick the ideas that you like.

1. Classroom robots _____ (give) complex sensors. They will hear us every time we talk in class.

2. Our class robot _____ (not / program) to understand voice commands in my language. When I need help, I will have to speak English.

3. Our robot _____ (teach) voice recognition. It will know my voice. When I need the robot's help, it will come to me.

4. Our class robot _____ (not / make) with just two mechanical arms. It'll have *lots* of arms.

5. The class robot _____ (train) in facial recognition. It will know when I am confused.

**12** **Play a game.** Use the game board on page 171. Play with a friend. Take turns. Predict what classroom robots and home robots will be like.

Robots will be trained to give us chocolate in class.

Oh, I definitely want a robot like that!

Heads=
1 space

Tails=
2 spaces

# Meet the Bots

Many people know that robots explore space and build things in factories. But did you know that there are many other kinds of robots? Let's meet some of these 'bots' and find out what they do.

Social robots are very popular. Wakamaru, a Japanese android robot, acts as a companion to elderly and disabled people. It can be programmed to remind people to take their medicine and it can also call for help in an emergency. Robovie II helps people go shopping. Domestic robots (robots that clean your house) are very popular today, but they can be very expensive!

Medical robots are extremely important in modern medicine. With the da Vinci Surgical System, the doctor sits several feet away from the patient and controls the robot's every move. The HeartLander can do heart surgery. Thanks to robotics engineers, we also have prosthetic hands that work like human hands.

Service robots help in emergencies. The VGTV is a tiny vehicle that can rescue people who are trapped under fallen buildings. These robots use sensors to discover who is trapped and then they send photos to the rescuers - all by remote control.

Explorer robots are incredibly useful, too. The Groundwater Voyager makes maps of underwater caves. And two Mars rovers, Opportunity and Curiosity, are exploring Mars. Amazing! What will future bots do?

**A restaurant in China has robot waiters! They even smile when they visit the tables.**

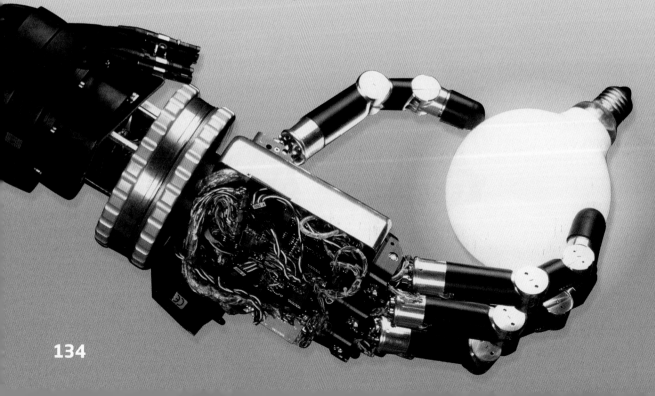

**14** **Tick T for *True* or F for *False*.**

1. Domestic robots are very expensive.     (T) (F)

2. Prosthetic hands are identical to real hands.     (T) (F)

3. Robotics engineers are people who design robots.     (T) (F)

4. The HeartLander rescues people in buildings.     (T) (F)

**15** **Complete the table.** Write what each robot does.
Tick what kind of robot it is.

|  | Function | Social | Medical | Service | Explorer |
|---|---|---|---|---|---|
| **Wakamaru** | It's a companion. | ✓ |  |  |  |
| **Robovie II** |  |  |  |  |  |
| **da Vinci** |  |  |  |  |  |
| **VGTV** |  |  |  |  |  |
| **Groundwater Voyager** |  |  |  |  |  |

**16** **Work with a friend.** Discuss which type of 'bot' is the most …

useful.      interesting.

complex.      unnecessary.

I think medical robots are the most useful.

Really? They are the most complex, but I think social robots are the most useful.

Why?

## Paragraphs of Advantages and Disadvantages

When you write a paragraph of advantages and disadvantages, you should include at least two advantages and two disadvantages. To make your views clear, use expressions like *on the one hand, on the other hand, one (dis)advantage is ...* and *another (dis)advantage is ...*

**17** **Read.** Read the paragraph. Underline the expressions that show advantages and disadvantages.

### Future bots: ready or not?

Today, bots are programmed and controlled by humans. But scientists are studying 'artificial intelligence' (AI) robots. These robots will be able to think for themselves and do things without us. On the one hand, this is positive. For example, if an explorer robot finds something interesting in space, it can make a decision about it. Another advantage is that when a social robot breaks, it will know how to fix itself. On the other hand, there are risks. Are we ready for robots that can think by themselves? One disadvantage is that they might do things we don't want them to do. For example, they might send emails that are supposed to be from us! Another disadvantage is that AI bots won't know about behaviour. They will need to be taught that some things are wrong, like stealing. If bots become too independent, the human world could become like a crazy science fiction film!

**18** **Write.** Write about the advantages and disadvantages of social robots as companions. Include two advantages and two disadvantages.

**19** **Work in a small group.** Share your writing.

# Mission

## Use technology wisely.

- Work in a small group. What technology do you use every day?

- How does technology help us? What are some disadvantages of technology? Make two lists. Write your best ideas in the box.

'From earliest times, humans had tools like hammers that extended our physical self. Today's technology extends our mental self. It's changing the way we experience the world.'

**Amber Case**
**Cyborg Anthropologist**
Emerging Explorer

> I use my phone every day.  I can talk to my
>
> brother overseas.
>
>
>

- Work with another group. Share your lists. Are they the same or different? Which ideas does everyone like best?

## 20 Design a robot.

1. Research personal robots.

2. Work in a small group. Imagine you could have a personal robot. Decide on some functions that you would like your personal robot to have.

3. Design a robot.

   a. Make a drawing of the robot.

   b. Label the features.

   c. Add information that explains what your new robot and its parts will look like.

   d. Discuss how your invention could have a positive impact.

4. Prepare a second drawing showing the robot doing its job.

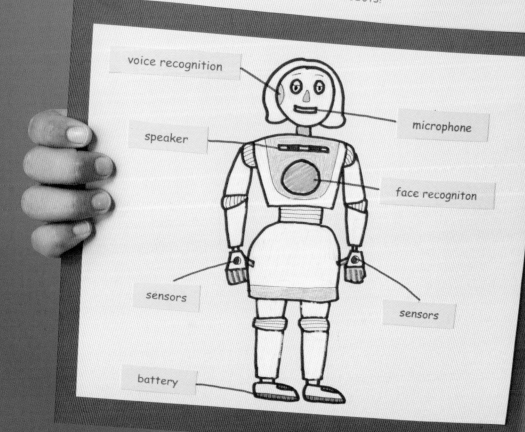

## Our Personal Robot

Our personal bot teaches you a new language. It's got speech recognition and facial recognition, so it recognises your face or your voice when you ta to it. This robot can recognise pictures and objects. So if you show it a mo phone, it will tell you how to say 'mobile phone' in English (or another langua It's got voice recognition, so it can correct your pronunciation, too. The best thing is that our bot tells jokes and sings songs! Our bot is a woman, but there are more designs, including animal robots!

voice recognition

speaker

microphone

face recogniton

sensors

sensors

battery

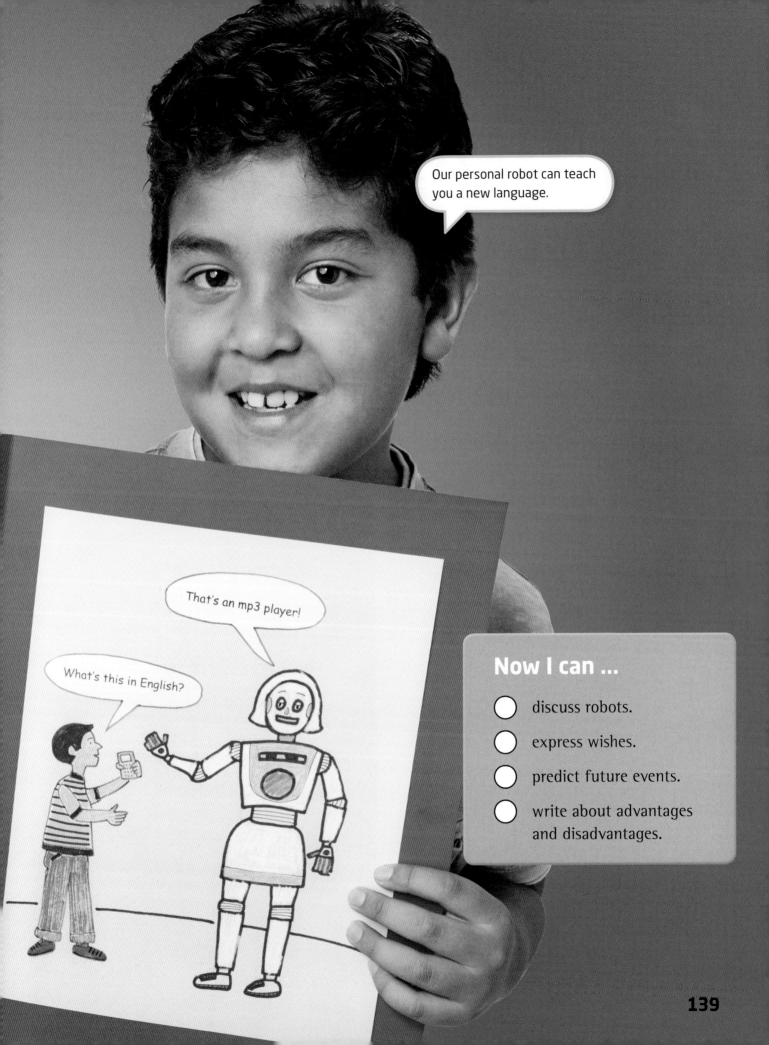

Our personal robot can teach you a new language.

That's an mp3 player!

What's this in English?

## Now I can ...

- ○ discuss robots.
- ○ express wishes.
- ○ predict future events.
- ○ write about advantages and disadvantages.

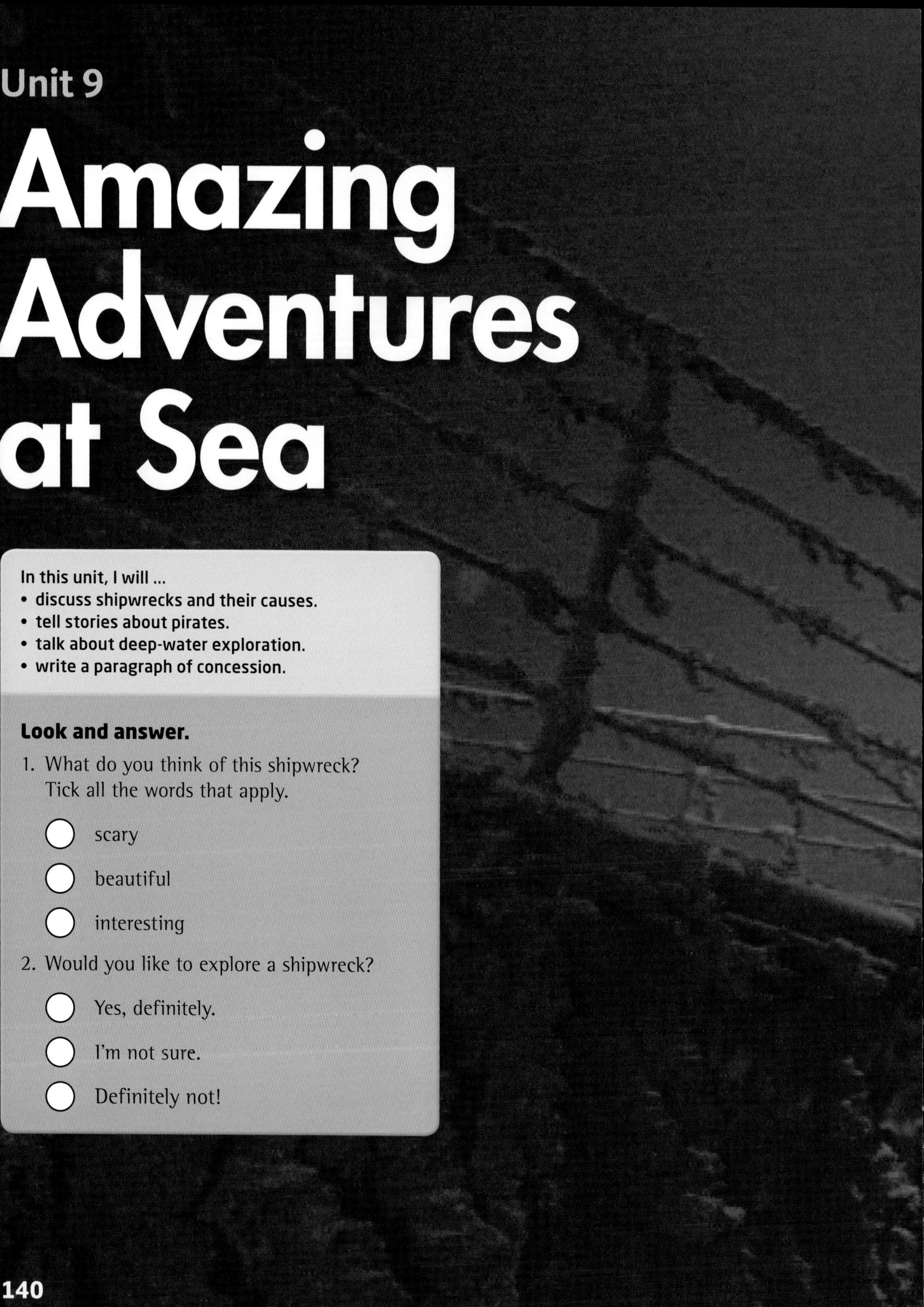

# Unit 9

# Amazing Adventures at Sea

**In this unit, I will ...**
- discuss shipwrecks and their causes.
- tell stories about pirates.
- talk about deep-water exploration.
- write a paragraph of concession.

## Look and answer.

1. What do you think of this shipwreck?
   Tick all the words that apply.

   ◯ scary

   ◯ beautiful

   ◯ interesting

2. Would you like to explore a shipwreck?

   ◯ Yes, definitely.

   ◯ I'm not sure.

   ◯ Definitely not!

*Titanic* shipwreck

**1** **Listen and read.** TR: B31

**2** **Listen and repeat.** TR: B32

More than a million **shipwrecks** lie on the ocean floor today. Many ships **sank** in bad weather, like the *Santa Margarita*, which was hit by a hurricane in 1622. What caused other shipwrecks?

Many centuries ago, ships carried **cargo** to sell to other countries. Ships also carried **weapons** because they were often attacked. In 1804, the Spanish ship *Nuestra Señora de las Mercedes* was attacked and exploded in a naval battle. It sank with over half a million **silver** coins.

**Pirates** were a big problem. In 1717, a famous pirate called Blackbeard **captured** the French ship *La Concorde*. By 1718, Blackbeard was **captain** of four stolen ships and had captured over 300 **sailors**! According to **legend**, he buried many treasures, but they have never been found.

The most famous modern shipwreck is the *Titanic*, which hit an **iceberg** and sank in 1912. There weren't enough **lifeboats** on board and over 1,500 people **drowned**, including most of the male **passengers** and **crew**. James Cameron, the director of the film *Titanic*, has **dived** down to the shipwreck's site more than 30 times.

a pirate

weapons

142

**3** **Work with a friend.** What did you learn? Ask and answer.

How many shipwrecks are on the ocean floor?

More than a million.

143

# Blackbeard

*Blackbeard, Blackbeard,*
*where's your silver now?*
*You've buried lots of treasure*
*that has never been found.*
*Blackbeard, Blackbeard,*
*I am going down*
*to the bottom of the sea*
*where treasure might be found.*

*I'm not afraid of icebergs. I'm not afraid of drowning.*
*I'm the bravest sailor for miles and miles around!*
*As soon as I'm a captain, with cargo and a crew,*
*I'll find your treasure deep in the sea so blue!*

*CHORUS*

*Local legend said there's a shipwreck nearby.*
*As soon as I am ready, I'm going there.*
*I love sunken treasure like flowers love the rain.*
*I'm going to dive down again and again.*

*Heave-ho! Here we go!*
*Get the silver! Get the gold!*
*Heave-ho! Here we go!*
*Get the treasure down below!*

*CHORUS*

*Blackbeard, Blackbeard, where's your silver now?*

**5** **Tick T for *True* or F for *False*.**

1. No one has found Blackbeard's treasure. (T) (F)

2. The singer has been looking for it. (T) (F)

3. Write a new title for the song.

_____

As soon as the *Santa Margarita* sank, people began looking for the silver.
Water poured into the *Titanic* **as soon as** it hit the iceberg.

**6** **Read and write.** Read the sentences. Write *1* above the action that happened first. Write *2* above the action that happened next. Rewrite and join the sentences.

       1                                2

1. A member of the crew saw the iceberg. He informed the captain.

   As soon as a member of the crew saw the iceberg, he informed the captain.

2. The sailors heard about the iceberg. They tried to sail in a different direction.

   _____

3. The side of the *Titanic* was damaged. The ship hit the iceberg.

   _____

4. The water entered. The ship began to sink.

   _____

5. The ship began to sink. Many people fell into the freezing cold water.

   _____

**7** **What about you?** Work in pairs. Ask the questions. Write answers in the table.

| What did you do as soon as you ... | Me | My friend |
|---|---|---|
| 1. finished breakfast today? | | |
| 2. finished lunch yesterday? | | |
| 3. left school yesterday? | | |
| 4. finished dinner last night? | | |
| 5. went to bed last night? | | |
| 6. woke up this morning? | | |
| 7. had breakfast yesterday? | | |
| 8. left home this morning? | | |

**8** **Work in a new group.** Read and discuss. Compare your activities. Were they the same or different?

What did you do as soon as you finished lunch yesterday?

I sent an email. What about you?

**9** **Listen and repeat.** Underline the correct word. TR: B35

correct          incorrect          safe          unsafe

legal          illegal          possible          impossible

1. Captains shouldn't put a lot of cargo on ships. The ships might sink. It is **safe / unsafe**.

2. These days it is **legal / illegal** to sail without a list of passengers. Captains have to have a list of everyone who is on the ship.

3. It is **possible / impossible** to know what happened to some ships. We have found lots of information at the shipwrecks.

4. According to legend, Blackbeard used to decorate his ships with human bones. That's **correct / incorrect**. Of course he didn't do that!

**10** **Listen and stick.** Tell your friend what each sign means. TR: B36

When you are on a ship, life jackets keep you safe.

That's right. Stick *safe* under picture 1.

**It is** important / useful / necessary / helpful **to** know how to swim.
**It is not** legal / safe / right **to** take artefacts from this shipwreck.
**It is** illegal / unsafe **to** be a pirate.

## 11 Read and write.

| | | |
|---|---|---|
| wrong / throw | impossible / know | important / wear |
| ~~interesting / dive~~ | illegal / sail | unsafe / swim |

1. _____It is interesting to dive_____ near shipwrecks. They are amazing

    habitats for sea creatures.

2. _____ a life jacket when you go sailing.

3. _____ how many people died on the *Doña*

    *Maria*. There wasn't a passenger list.

4. _____ without a licence. But some people

    still do it.

5. _____ rubbish in the sea.

6. _____ with sharks.

## 12 Play a game. Cut out the cards on page 173 and use the game board
on page 175. Place the cards face down in a pile. Work in a small group.
Take turns. Follow the route, pick a card and make a sentence.

It is exciting to explore shipwrecks.

My turn!

# Journey to the Bottom of the Earth

James Cameron, the famous explorer and film director, travelled to the deepest point of the Mariana Trench – the Challenger Deep – on 26th March, 2012. At about 11,000 metres (about 36,000 feet) below sea level, this is the deepest point on Earth. Since childhood, Cameron has wanted to dive and explore the ocean. Now he has reached the deepest point in the ocean. Alone.

The Mariana Trench is perhaps the most isolated place on the planet. Because of its extreme depth, the pressure at the bottom of the Mariana Trench is incredibly strong. The temperature is just a few degrees above freezing and the place is always in darkness. Although two explorers went there in 1960, Cameron was the first to film this strange, dark place.

For this incredible expedition, Cameron travelled in a submersible called the *DEEPSEA CHALLENGER*. It was 7.3 metres (24 feet) long and 1.09 metres (43 inches) wide – so small that Cameron could hardly move. Yet the sub was powerful enough to reach the bottom of the ocean in just two hours and 36 minutes and ascend in 70 minutes! In the *DEEPSEA CHALLENGER*, Cameron spent three hours filming the bottom of the ocean while its mechanical arms picked up rocks and animals.

We know less about the deepest points on our planet than we do about the surface of Mars. But the samples Cameron collected will give scientists a lot of information. When they analyse the rocks, they might discover more about the shape of the land and the earthquakes that cause tsunamis. And by studying the organisms that survive there, perhaps scientists can even learn more about how life began!

In the *DEEPSEA CHALLENGER*, all the water vapour from Cameron's breath was condensed and stored in a plastic bag so that Cameron could drink it in an emergency!

JAPAN

CHINA

PHILIPPINES

GUAM

INDONESIA

PAPUA NEW GUINEA

Mariana Trench

**14** **Read.** (Circle) the answer.

1. Cameron was the _____ person to dive to the

    Mariana Trench.

    a. first          b. second          c. third

2. He had dreamt about this journey since he was _____ .

    a. born          b. a boy          c. 15 years old

3. There wasn't _____ room inside the *DEEPSEA CHALLENGER*.

    a. any          b. much          c. enough

4. The rocks from the Mariana Trench could teach us about _____ .

    a. earthquakes     b. organisms     c. the next dive

**15** **Re-read the text.** Complete the Fact File.

THE *DEEPSEA CHALLENGER*

Length _____

Width _____

Depth travelled _____

Descent time _____

Ascent time _____

**16** **Work in pairs.** Role play an interview with
James Cameron. Ask and answer questions about
these topics.

James Cameron                          *DEEPSEA CHALLENGER*
Journey to the Mariana Trench          Importance of the expedition
Mariana Trench

## Paragraphs of Concession

In a paragraph of concession, you discuss opinions. You also accept that different points of view may be partially correct. When you use concession, you can use words such as *even though*, *granted that*, *although* or *while it may be true*.

**17** **Read.** Underline the words of concession used in this paragraph.

## Whose treasure is it?

In 2007, an American shipwreck salvage company discovered more than 500,000 silver coins in a shipwreck in the Atlantic Ocean. The silver is from the Nuestra Señora de las Mercedes, a Spanish ship that sank when it was attacked in 1804. Who does the treasure belong to today? The Spanish government says that the silver is theirs, but is it? While it may be true that the ship was Spanish, it was carrying the silver from Peru. And the Peruvian government says the silver is theirs because the coins were made with Peruvian silver. So, whose is it? Although the explorers who discovered the treasure are from the USA, there is an agreement between the USA and Spain that says all silver from Spanish shipwrecks has to go back to Spain. So even though three countries wanted this treasure, it now belongs to Spain.

**18** **Write.** Write about the objects found in the *Titanic* shipwreck. Do the objects belong to the explorers, the relatives of survivors or museums? Use expressions of concession.

**19** **Work in a small group.** Share your writing.

# NATIONAL GEOGRAPHIC
# Mission

## Be a lifelong learner.

- What do you dream of doing?

- How can you prepare for it? Think of ideas. Make notes in the box.

*'There are thousands of undiscovered shipwrecks and ancient sites in Cuba. It's an immense field of work waiting for archaeologists to explore.'*

**Daniel Torres Etayo**
**Archaeologist**
Emerging Explorer

I'd like to be an underwater explorer. First,

I must learn to swim.

Work with a friend. Share your ideas.
Are they the same or different?

**Havana, Cuba**

RAMAC/GPR

153

## 20 Plan your first exploration.

1. Work with a friend. Choose something or somewhere that you would like to explore together.

2. Plan your first exploration.

   a. What do you need to know about the topic before you go on your expedition? Make a list. Discuss how you can research more information.

   b. Choose some people (for example, scientists) who should go with you on your trip.

   c. List what you need to take with you on your trip.

3. Make a poster.

We're planning a trip to the Caribbean to find an old shipwreck. It was one of Blackbeard's ships!

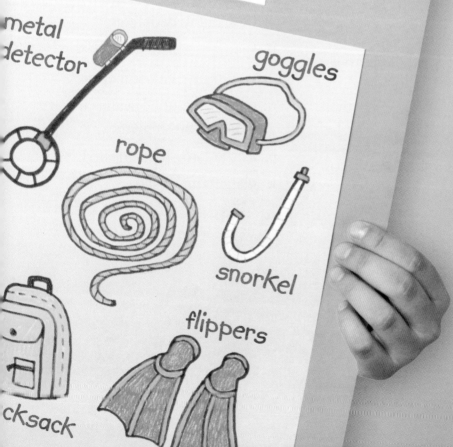

Equipment

metal detector

goggles

rope

snorkel

flippers

cksack

## Now I can ...

○ discuss shipwrecks and their causes.

○ tell stories about pirates.

○ talk about deep-water exploration.

○ write a paragraph of concession.

# Review

**1** **Listen to the story.** Tick the ship. TR: B39

| | The *Doña Paz* | The *Vector* | Neither |
|---|---|---|---|
| 1. Attacked by pirates | | | ✓ |
| 2. Crossed the ocean in 1987 | | | |
| 3. Carried oil | | | |
| 4. Carried weapons and silver | | | |
| 5. Had too many passengers on board | | | |
| 6. Sank | | | |
| 7. Sailors died in the fire | | | |
| 8. Captain didn't have a licence. | | | |

**2** **Listen again.** Match. TR: B40

1. Shipwrecks make Amy feel ____

2. The *Doña Paz* captain was wrong. He allowed too many passengers on board. It was ____

3. The fire started as soon ____

4. It's impossible to know ____

5. Ben wishes that he ____

6. Amy wishes that he ____

a. how many people died.

b. sad.

c. would be quiet sometimes.

d. could dive underwater and explore the shipwreck.

e. as the two ships crashed.

f. illegal and unsafe.

**3** **Work with a friend.** Imagine you were on board the *Vector* or the *Doña Paz*. Describe what happened. Take turns. Ask and answer questions.

**4  Read.** Look at the pictures. Match the sentence halves.

 **Wear It!**   **Do Not Touch!**   **No Crossing!**

1. A headlamp _____

2. Stalactites and stalagmites __ _

3. This stream _____

4. One day this robot _____

5. Tunnels _____

a. will be programmed to think for itself.

b. can't be crossed.

c. must be worn in the cave.

d. mustn't be touched.

e. can be found underground.

**5  Write.** Choose four objects from the list. Write clues for your friend.

| | |
|---|---|
| bat | pirate |
| caves | safety equipment |
| iceberg | remote control |
| information | science fiction films |
| painting | underwater robots |

| | | | |
|---|---|---|---|
| must (not) be | has to be | ascend | find |
| can be | will be | control | touch |
| can't be | won't be | descend | use |

*This can be used to turn off the TV.*
*These robots descend to the bottom of the sea.*

**6  Work in a group.** Take turns. Read your clues to your friends. Can they guess? Win a point for each correct guess!

# Let's Talk

## See what I mean?

**I will ...**
- open a conversation.
- state an opinion and clarify it.
- check understanding.
- confirm an opinion.

**1** **Listen and read.** TR: B41

Ahmed: **You know**, I don't think we need to practise handwriting any more. In the future, we won't need to write.

Yusef: **Really**? **Why do you say that**?

Ahmed: **Well**, in the future we'll just talk to the computer and it will write for us! **I mean**, no one is going to write by hand in a few years. So, it doesn't make sense to practise handwriting now. **See what I mean**?

Yusef: **What**? **Are you saying that** we won't need to write any notes either? No writing at all?

Ahmed: Well, of course people will write by hand sometimes! **What I mean is** ...

| You know, You know what? | Really? Why do you say that? You think so? Why's that? | Well, ... I mean, ... You see, ... | See what I mean? Do you see what I mean?<br><br>What I mean is ... What I meant was ... | What? Are you saying that ___ ? So you're saying that ___ ? So are you saying that ___ ? |
|---|---|---|---|---|

**2** **Work with a friend.** Use the expressions in the table. Discuss a future change that you believe will happen.

# Please have a look.

I will ...
- refer to visuals in a presentation.
- invite questions from the audience.
- end a presentation.

**3** **Listen and read.** TR: B42

Natalie: **Please have a look at** our poster. **This shows** something you can make for your home.

Emily: **You'll notice that** it's made from just a simple object.

Natalie: This is a good example of recycling.

Emily: Now, **would anyone like to ask any questions**?

Natalie: OK, **that concludes our presentation**.

Emily: And **our time's up**. **Thanks for listening**, everyone.

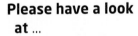

| **Please have a look at** ... | **You'll notice that** ... | **Would anyone like to ask any questions**? | **Thanks for listening**. |
|---|---|---|---|
| Now, let's look at ...<br>Here's a picture of ...<br>**This** table **shows** ... | If you look closely, you'll see that ...<br>As you can see, ... | Are there any questions?<br>Has anyone got any questions? | **That concludes our presentation**.<br>**Our time's up**. |

**4** **Listen.** You will hear two discussions. What are the two students showing the class? Circle the answer. TR: B43

1.    a. a poster    b. a book    c. some photos    d. an invention or model

2.    a. a poster    b. a book    c. some photos    d. an invention or model

**5** **Work in pairs.** Prepare and practise presentations.

1. You are showing the class something you made using recycled materials.

2. You are showing the class a poster with photos from an archaeological site.

3. You are showing the class an invention.

**159**

# Irregular Verbs

| Infinitive | Past Simple | Past Participle | Infinitive | Past Simple | Past Participle |
|---|---|---|---|---|---|
| be | was/were | been | lie | lay | lain |
| beat | beat | beaten | light | lit | lit |
| become | became | become | lose | lost | lost |
| begin | began | begun | make | made | made |
| bend | bent | bent | meet | met | met |
| bite | bit | bitten | pay | paid | paid |
| bleed | bled | bled | put | put | put |
| blow | blew | blown | read | read | read |
| break | broke | broken | ride | rode | ridden |
| bring | brought | brought | ring | rang | rung |
| build | built | built | rise | rose | risen |
| buy | bought | bought | run | ran | run |
| catch | caught | caught | say | said | said |
| choose | chose | chosen | see | saw | seen |
| come | came | come | sell | sold | sold |
| cost | cost | cost | send | sent | sent |
| cut | cut | cut | set | set | set |
| dig | dug | dug | sew | sewed | sewn |
| do | did | done | shake | shook | shaken |
| draw | drew | drawn | shine | shone | shone |
| drink | drank | drunk | show | showed | shown |
| drive | drove | driven | shut | shut | shut |
| eat | ate | eaten | sing | sang | sung |
| fall | fell | fallen | sink | sank | sunk |
| feed | fed | fed | sit | sat | sat |
| feel | felt | felt | sleep | slept | slept |
| fight | fought | fought | slide | slid | slid |
| find | found | found | speak | spoke | spoken |
| fly | flew | flown | spend | spent | spent |
| forget | forgot | forgotten | spin | spun | spun |
| forgive | forgave | forgiven | stand | stood | stood |
| freeze | froze | frozen | steal | stole | stolen |
| get | got | got | stick | stuck | stuck |
| give | gave | given | sting | stung | stung |
| go | went | gone | stink | stank | stunk |
| grow | grew | grown | sweep | swept | swept |
| hang | hung | hung | swim | swam | swum |
| have | had | had | swing | swung | swung |
| hear | heard | heard | take | took | taken |
| hide | hid | hidden | teach | taught | taught |
| hit | hit | hit | tear | tore | torn |
| hold | held | held | tell | told | told |
| hurt | hurt | hurt | think | thought | thought |
| keep | kept | kept | throw | threw | thrown |
| know | knew | known | understand | understood | understood |
| learn | learnt | learnt | wake up | woke up | woken up |
| leave | left | left | wear | wore | worn |
| lend | lent | lent | win | won | won |
| let | let | let | write | wrote | written |

Where do cacao trees grow?

Why was a recipe printed? (So that …)

Name three ingredients in chocolate.

Go back two spaces!

When is International Chocolate Day?

Name one type of chocolate filling.

Go back two spaces!

Why was sugar added to chocolate? (So that …)

How many types of chocolate bars are there today?

Go back two spaces!

When was the first chocolate bar made?

Why did Joseph Fry add new ingredients to chocolate? (So that …)

Go forward one space!

What do farmers open to take out cacao seeds?

What's your favourite type of chocolate?

Go forward one space!

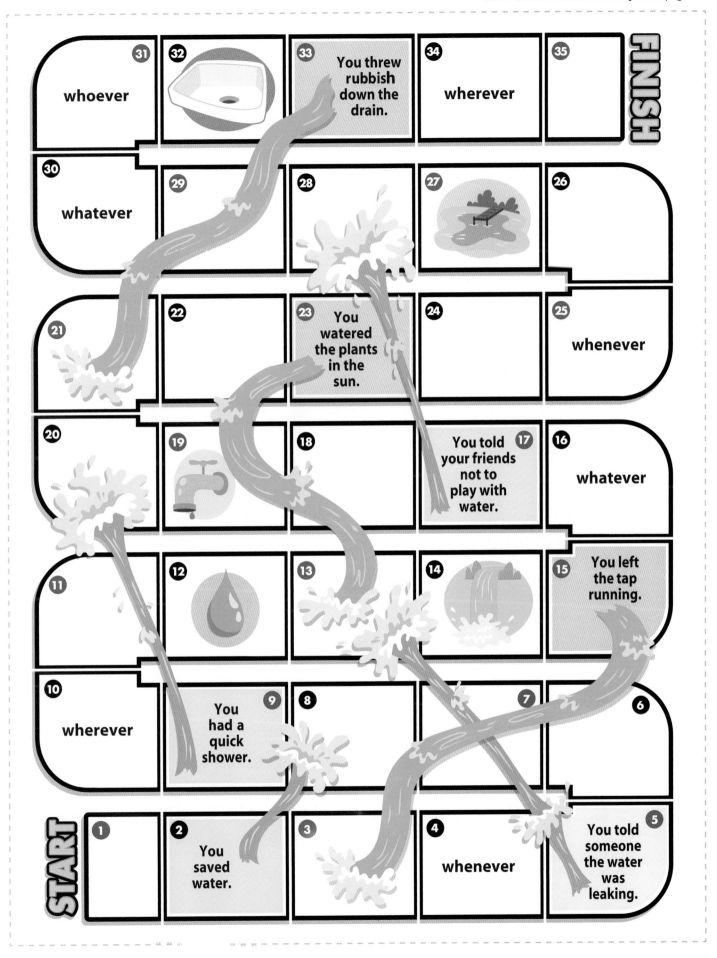

FINISH

31 whoever

32

33 You threw rubbish down the drain.

34 wherever

35

30 whatever

29

28

27

26

21

22

23 You watered the plants in the sun.

24

25 whenever

20

19

18

17 You told your friends not to play with water.

16 whatever

11

12

13

14

15 You left the tap running.

10 wherever

9 You had a quick shower.

8

7

6

START

1

2 You saved water.

3

4 whenever

5 You told someone the water was leaking.

163

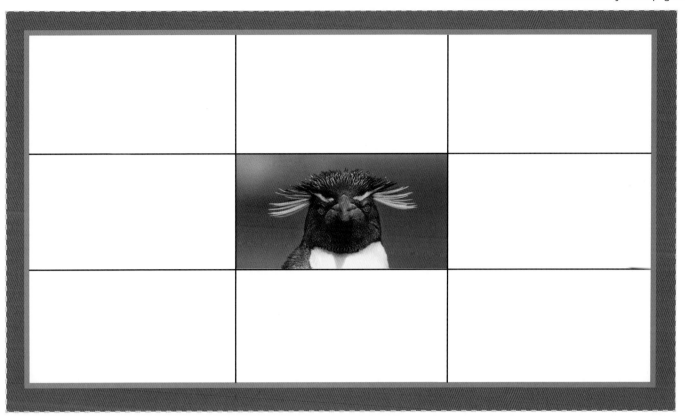

| | |
|---|---|
| **Where is the computer store?** | **Can you show me your rucksack?** |
| **Where can I buy this phone?** | **Can I have a bicycle for my birthday?** |
| **Where can I buy a toy car like this?** | **Can you help me?** |
| **What do we need to buy next?** | **Do you like these jeans?** |
| **How much do these trainers cost?** | **Have you got a tablet?** |
| **Can I help you?** | **Have you got a TV with a large screen?** |

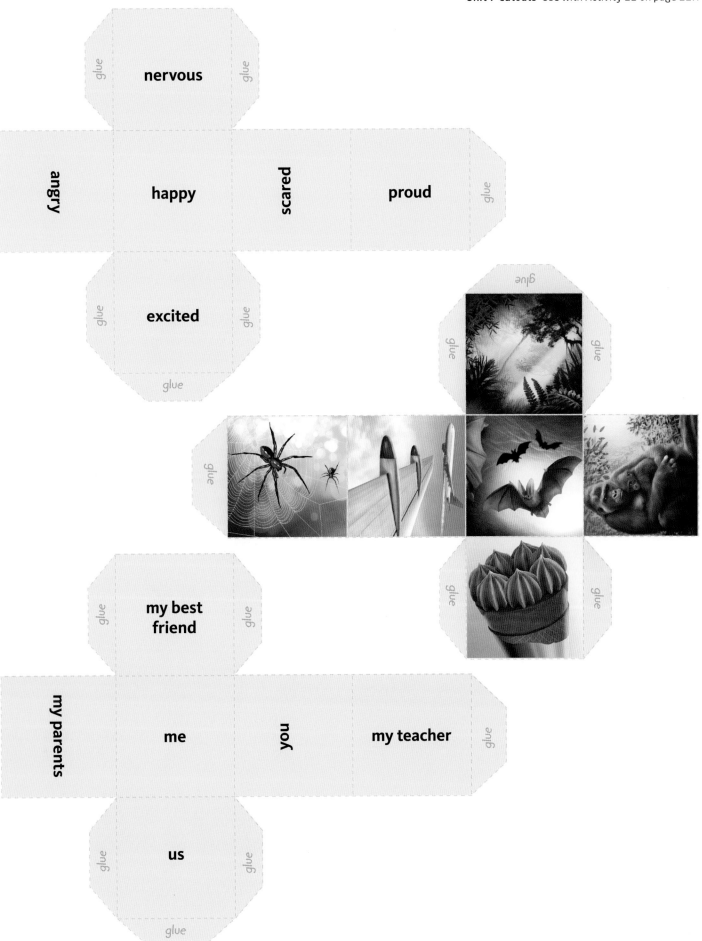

nervous

angry

happy

scared

proud

excited

my best friend

my parents

me

you

my teacher

us

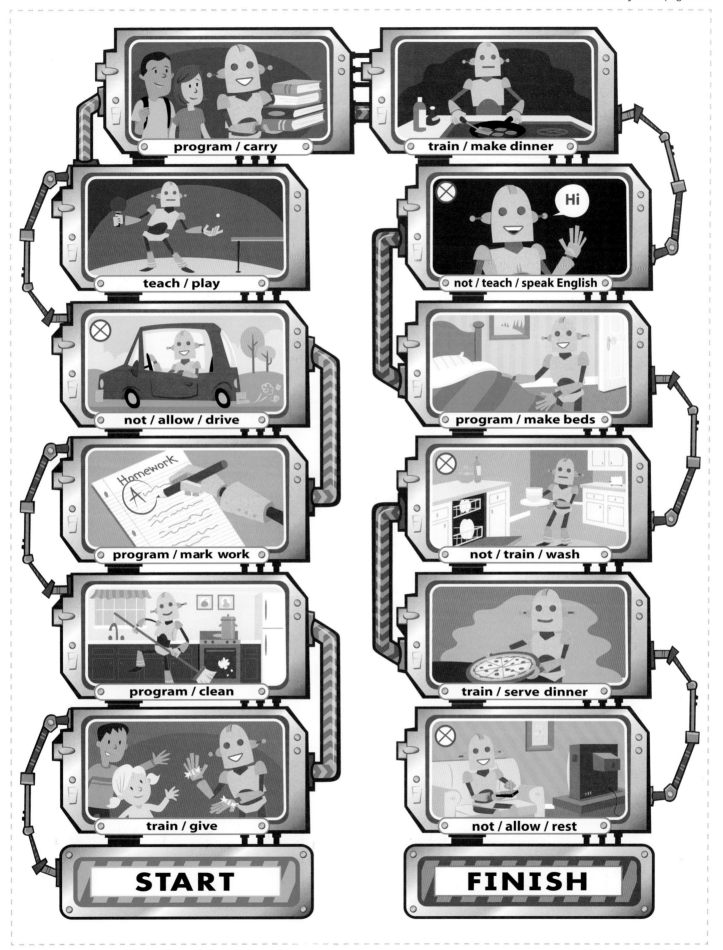

**You are captured by pirates.**
**Go back three spaces.**

**Sharks are attacking your ship.**
**Miss a turn.**

| important /<br>wear life jacket | interesting /<br>learn about |
| important /<br>wear bike helmet | interesting /<br>discover |

**You find some treasure!**
**Move forward three spaces.**

**There is a big storm.**
**Go back two spaces.**

| important /<br>listen to | interesting /<br>read about |
| important /<br>study English | possible / drown |

**The wind is blowing**
**in the right direction.**
**Move forward two spaces.**

**Your ship has a leak.**
**Miss a turn.**

| unsafe /<br>swim alone | possible /<br>discover creatures |
| unsafe /<br>go out late | impossible / know |

**You capture a famous pirate.**
**Move forward two spaces.**

**Lots of your sailors are sick.**
**Go back two spaces.**

| unsafe / run | impossible / go |
| unsafe /<br>try to save a friend<br>in the water | illegal /<br>take artefacts |

| useful / have | useful / wear | necessary / have | illegal / cross |
| necessary / study | exciting / explore | exciting / watch | fun / make |
| right / save | not right / waste | not right / pollute | fun / watch |
| right / recycle | useful / know | | |

## Unit 1
### stickers

## Unit 2
### stickers

| were sick | lived close by | same family | were rich | ate meat |
| --- | --- | --- | --- | --- |
| DNA test | samples | CT scan | artefacts | the site |

## Unit 3
### stickers

## Unit 4
### stickers

## Unit 5
### stickers